Harrier
Vertical Velocity Warfare

KEY
Books

HISTORIC MILITARY AIRCRAFT SERIES, VOLUME 34

Published by Key Books
An imprint of Key Publishing Ltd
PO Box 100
Stamford
Lincs PE9 1XQ

www.keypublishing.com

Original edition published as *Aeroplane Icons: Hawker Harrier*
© 2015, edited by Tim McLelland

This edition © 2023

ISBN 978 1 80282 752 1

Typeset by SJmagic DESIGN SERVICES, India.

Contents

Introduction 4

Chapter 1 Perpendicular Propulsion 5

Chapter 2 Supersonic Sideline 21

Chapter 3 Combat Considerations 41

Chapter 4 Maritime Manoeuvrings 65

Chapter 5 Second Generation Woes 79

Introduction

To describe the Harrier as a remarkable warplane would be an understatement. Although its ability to take off and land vertically was not unique, it was the only aircraft that ever successfully translated this asset into a fully functional combat capability, and it is only half a century later that another aircraft has emerged that shares the same abilities. But of course, the F-35 is a very different machine, endowed with technological advances that could not have even been imagined when the Harrier was on the proverbial drawing board. Designed as a ground attack aircraft that would be virtually immune from the risk of attack from Soviet forces, the Harrier became a supremely capable Cold War fighter and bomber, eagerly embraced not only by Britain's Royal Air Force (RAF) and Royal Navy, but also by the mighty United States Marine Corps (USMC), together with a number of export customers around the world. By any standards, the Harrier was a tremendous success, and its illustrious history is perhaps only marred by the way in which it was prematurely abandoned by the very nation that had created it, a victim of political cost cutting. This book takes a look at the history of the Harrier, tracing its origins and the fascinating story of how the Hawker P.1127 was developed into both the Kestrel and finally the Harrier, together with a look at the Harrier's more modern reincarnation as the American-inspired AV-8B.

Chapter 1

Perpendicular Propulsion

Development of the vertical take-off concept

It was during World War Two that Nazi Germany first explored the possibility of creating a combat aircraft that could operate independently of fixed runways, safe from the risk of destruction by enemy forces. Erich Bachem was credited with the design of the Ba349 'Natter', a bizarre rocket-powered interceptor that was intended to give the Luftwaffe a means of successfully defending the Reich from relentless Allied bombing. The radical design of the Natter was to have given Germany an interceptor that would be completely mobile, capable of being launched from any suitable clearing amongst the safety of woodland camouflage where the chances of locating and destroying it prior to launch were almost nil. Launched vertically under radio control, the diminutive wooden-built interceptor would rocket upwards from its support tower and head directly towards its target; at that stage the pilot would resume direct control and fire a salvo of rockets at his target, after that he would use his fuel-starved aircraft to ram the enemy bomber before ejecting to return to the ground by parachute. The Natter was not the only vertical take-off and landing (VTOL) concept that Germany pursued. Amongst a variety of unusual and radical design proposals, one of the more bizarre was the Focke-Achgelis Fa.269, a piston-powered fighter that was to have been operated from Germany's merchant vessels. Unlike the Natter, the Fa.269 did not rely on rocket power to achieve vertical take-off but took advantage of another revolutionary idea that had emerged from many months of scientific research – thrust vectoring. The aircraft's two propellers, fixed aft of the wing, could power the aircraft for conventional flight, but thanks to some ingenious engineering work they could also be pivoted downwards, giving the aircraft an ability to take off (and land) vertically from the confines of the ship's deck. These two designs represented two very different means of achieving vertical take-off, but both concepts would re-emerge elsewhere in post-war years. Other ambitious designs were also being considered, such as the Focke-Wulf Triebflugel, a particularly unusual design that comprised three small jet engines fixed to wings that rotated about the aircraft's fuselage, combining the properties of jet thrust with the vertical lift of helicopter blades. Whether the concept would ever have worked is open to question but the Triebflugel – like all of the Luftwaffe's colourful concepts – illustrated that Germany was eager to get into the vertical take-off business as soon as it possibly could.

Across the Atlantic, the US military also understood VTOL's potential, and in 1951, the US Navy (USN) issued a requirement for a fleet fighter with VTOL capabilities that would be operated from the Navy's surface vessels. Precisely how much influence the wartime German designs might have had on the Navy's thinking is open to question but instead of pursuing the concept of an aircraft like the Fa.269, the Navy's interest was geared towards a tail-sitter design that would literally hang under its propeller and, after having clawed its way into the air, the aircraft would then rotate through 90 degrees into forward flight. Eventually a pair of designs emerged, these being the Lockheed XFV-1 (two prototypes) and the Convair XFY-1 (three prototypes), both powered by an Allison T40-a-14 turboprop engine driving huge contra-rotating propellers. Although these experimental aircraft were regarded as successful, the Navy abandoned its interest in the concept just two years later. The difficulties of the

Rolls-Royce's bizarre Thrust Measuring Rig (TMR) pictured during one of its test hovers at Hucknall. Although clumsy and cumbersome, the TMR did successfully demonstrate that a vehicle could be controlled purely through the use of jet lift, aided by reaction control vents with which to achieve roll, pitch and yaw. (*Aeroplane*)

The revolutionary Bachem Natter was in effect a controlled missile, but it was also the first practical application of vertical take-off and landing (VTOL) technology. (*Aeroplane*)

complicated transition to and from vertical flight were eventually sufficient to convince the Navy that an operational aircraft would be troublesome, and the designs did not offer any obvious means of easy development into a viable combat aircraft. It was Ryan Aeronautical Company that first explored the possibility of using jet thrust for VTOL and, by 1947, the San Diego company was busy developing a 'test rig' (powered by an Allison J33 turbojet) capable of hovering and manoeuvring with the aid of reaction controls. The Ryan test rig led to the receipt of a United States Air Force (USAF) contract for a 'proof-of-concept' aircraft, and, on 10 December 1955, the Ryan X-13 made its first (conventional) flight. Its single Rolls-Royce Avon turbojet delivered a thrust of 9,100lb and, with a full fuel load, the X-13 was capable of operating for up to a maximum of just 12 minutes. Unlike the Navy's VTOL aircraft, the X-13 did not operate directly from the ground, and without any fixed landing gear, the aircraft was attached to an hydraulically operated ramp that raised the aircraft to its vertical launch position prior to release. In some respects, this made the X-13 even more difficult to handle than the Convair and Lockheed designs, but the X-13 was intended only to demonstrate the viability of jet lift and the X-13 achieved this aim. However, in much the same way as the Navy eventually lost interest in the concept, the USAF also shifted its attention to other projects.

Following the formation of the North Atlantic Treaty Organisation (NATO) in 1949, America began to develop a more active interest in European military thinking and ploughed huge amounts of money into NATO's structure at the start of what had become the Cold War. Many long-established wartime airfields were already scattered around West Germany, but their proximity to the Soviet border made them less than ideal locations. Alternative sites had to be created further west, and with funding supplied by America, huge new airfields began to appear from where American and NATO forces could bring in fast and capable aircraft to the new front line. Destroying these sites would be the Soviet's primary aim and even at some distance from the East-West border, sufficient enemy air assets could be directed against

Tom Brooke-Smith brings the diminutive SC.1 into the hover for a vertical landing during handling trials at RAE Bedford. After initial trials, both SC.1s were assigned to research flying at Bedford until retirement. The two SC.1 aircraft demonstrated that vertical lift engines provided an effective means of achieving VTOL, but when compared to vectored thrust, the system was less efficient and far less reliable. Rolls-Royce maintained an active interest in the concept but ultimately it was Bristol's vectored-thrust engine that held far more potential. (*Aeroplane*)

these airfields to quickly render them useless – probably on the very first day of any confrontation. Combat aircraft had been designed with their weapon-carrying abilities in mind, but no concessions had been made to their airfield performance. They all required long runways, and nobody was willing to grapple with the question of how NATO could continue to operate its fighter and attack aircraft if these runways were disabled or destroyed. However, a Frenchman was addressing this very issue. Michel Wibault was a respected aviation designer having been responsible for the creation of many pre-war metal-built monoplanes and the production of many unusual and imaginative design concepts. During February 1956, he approached the French Air Ministry in Paris with a typically revolutionary design in the shape of a small swept-wing aircraft that would be suitable as the basis for a new light attack aircraft. Unusually, instead of featuring a conventional exhaust emerging from the rear of the aircraft, Wibault's design embraced a new concept of vectored jet thrust, using an 8,000hp Bristol BE.25 Orion turboprop engine to power four centrifugal blower units positioned at right angles to the aircraft's fore and aft datum line. By shifting (vectoring) the position of these blowers from horizontal to vertical, the aircraft would be capable of taking off and landing vertically. The French Air Ministry was initially inclined to dismiss the idea as impractical, but Wibault was advised to approach the Mutual Weapons Development Program (MWDP), which was being funded by the United States, and also to approach NATO's Advisory Group for

Aeronautical Research and Development (AGARD). The MWDP's Colonel Willis 'Bill' Chapman studied the proposal with interest and instructed a team of experts to thoroughly investigate Wibault's idea. The MWDP was already working with Bristol Engines in the UK (developing the Orpheus turbojet for the Fiat G.91), and so it seemed logical to Chapman that the matter should be referred to that company's technical director, Sir Stanley Hooker.

Sir Stanley Hooker had come to Bristol Engines from Rolls-Royce where he had already become an expert on engine design and development. Rolls-Royce had already taken a great interest in VTOL engine concepts and, in 1953, the company had produced the Thrust Measuring Rig (TMR), comprising two 5,000lb thrust Rolls-Royce Nene turbojets positioned at each end of a metal framework, with long pipes through which high pressure air was tapped from the engines to provide roll and pitch stability. The TMR demonstrated the viability of the jet lift concept and Britain's Ministry of Supply recognised this potential, issuing Specification ER.143 for a small VTOL aircraft that could investigate the potential of Rolls-Royce's RB.108 engines (developed from experience with

Sir Stanley Hooker, creator of the ingenious Pegasus engine, which enabled the Harrier family to be developed. (Brian Stanley Collection)

the TMR), and demonstrate how the powerplant could be incorporated into a fixed-wing aircraft. Belfast-based Short Brothers submitted a proposal to meet the specification, and this was eventually accepted, resulting in two prototypes of their diminutive SC.1 being ordered in August 1954.

The SC.1 was based around four RB.108 engines stacked vertically in the aircraft's fuselage with a further engine arranged to emerge almost horizontally from the rear of the fuselage. The first aircraft (XG900) made its first conventional flight on 2 April 1957 from Boscombe Down, powered only by a single rearwards-facing engine. On 23 May of the following year, the second aircraft (XG905) made its first tethered hover with lift engines installed. During April 1960, the SC.1 made its first transition to and from vertical and conventional flight regimes and during the SBAC show in September, Tom Brooke-Smith demonstrated the aircraft's full capabilities to the public. Testing continued but, on 2 October 1963, the aircraft's stabilisation system failed, and the test pilot (J. R. Green) was unable to assume manual control before the aircraft hit the ground and overturned, killing him. This was, in fact, the second British jet VTOL fatality as Rolls-Royce's second THR (XK426) had collided with a support gantry and had overturned at Hucknall on 27 November 1957, resulting in the death of its pilot (Wing Commander H. G. F. Larson). The SC.1 was eventually repaired and both airframes continued to provide valuable research data for many years, but with no practical application for jet lift technology in sight the SC.1 represented no more than an interesting episode in the story of VTOL development.

The development of Rolls-Royce's RB.108 had been watched with great interest by Bristol's Stanley Hooker. Rolls-Royce had patented the engine design and had effectively precluded any possibility of the concept being developed elsewhere. Although Hooker remained interested in VTOL, he was unable to pursue the concept with Bristol Engines, but when Chapman invited him to Paris in July 1956, he

Convair's XFY-1 Pogo represented one of the more obvious means of achieving VTOL, but it did not address the equally obvious difficulties of transitioning to and from vertical flight. Experience soon demonstrated that the tricky manoeuvre was barely within the skills of test pilots and could not be applied to an operational design. (US Navy)

was more than eager to learn more about Michel Wibault's proposal. Instead of a reliance upon vertical jet lift engines (which had to be carried as a very significant 'dead weight' in conventional flight), Wibault's single engine could provide both horizontal propulsion and jet lift. Hooker was mindful of the support given to Bristol Engines by the MWDP during the development of its Orpheus engine, and he accepted Chapman's invitation to give Wibault's idea a more detailed appraisal. After only a couple of weeks, Bristol had already identified ways in which the concept could be revised and refined. Most importantly, Wibault's centrifugal blower system was abandoned in favour of a less complicated means of directing flow from a central axial compressor through two rotating pipes emerging on each side of the aircraft fuselage. The remainder of the engine layout would function conventionally, with a standard horizontal exhaust at the rear. This inevitably meant that there would be insufficient vertical thrust to enable the aircraft to take off and land vertically, but it would give an aircraft a very useful short take-off capability. Bristol's Gordon Lewis then proposed linking a Bristol Orion engine to a large frontal fan from which high-pressure air could be directed to the left and right rotating nozzles, providing both vertical lift and/or horizontal thrust. This design (the BE.48) was the first in a series of developments that translated Wibault's idea into a viable propulsion system. Further studies suggested that the Orion engine should be replaced by the company's new Orpheus engine – a lighter (and potentially cheaper) engine that delivered a similar amount of thrust. It was established that by adding a turbine to the rear of this engine, the front high-pressure turbine could be powered through a linking shaft which could run through the existing high-pressure shaft inside the Orpheus. This would enable the elimination of the complicated reduction gearbox. The result was the more advanced Bristol BE.53 engine with an estimated vectored thrust of some 8,000lb.

During the 1957 Paris Air Show, the legendary Sir Sydney Camm (Hawker Aircraft's chief designer) met with Maj Gerard Morel, a French representative of both Hawker Aircraft and Bristol Engines. While observing a demonstration of SNECMA's unwieldy Atar test rig (similar to Rolls-Royce's TMR), Morel asked Camm whether he was aware of Bristol's work on the new BE.53 engine and its possible applications for future combat aircraft design. Camm knew nothing about the project but expressed some interest in the idea, and just a few days later, a full descriptive brochure arrived at Hawker's headquarters at Kingston-upon-Thames. Camm seriously doubted Bristol's claim that a developed engine might produce up to 11,000lb of thrust but he accepted that the engine did (at least in theory) offer the possibility of creating an aircraft with short take-off and landing (STOL) abilities. He instructed one of his senior design engineers (Ralph Hooper) to investigate the engine more thoroughly and consider what kind of aircraft might take advantage of the engine's unique properties. Hooper quickly concluded that the estimated thrust of the engine would be insufficient to enable any significant weapons load to

Above left: **Michael Wibault, the talented and respected French designer, who first proposed the revolutionary concept of vectored jet thrust. (Brian Stanley Collection)**

Above right: **Sir Sydney Camm, credited as the 'father' of the Harrier programme. (Brian Stanley Collection)**

be carried and he therefore proposed that the engine could power a small three-seat STOL battlefield liaison aircraft. The first design drawing for this aircraft was dated 28 June and was specified as the Hawker P.1127.

Initially, both Hooper and his engineering colleague John Fozard were not particularly enthusiastic about the P.1127, chiefly because of the BE.53 engine's thrust limitations. A subsequent design for a two-man aircraft (with revised intakes) offered the prospect of a slightly more practical aircraft, but it was agreed that developmental increases in weight would inevitably overtake engine performance, and in essence, it was only Hawker's increasingly desperate need for a future project that kept the idea alive rather than any real enthusiasm for the design (the company was struggling to find work following drastic reductions in defence procurement). A high-speed battlefield liaison aircraft was no Hurricane or Hunter, and in many respects P.1127 was an abstract design concept in need of a practical application, rather than vice versa. But everything changed drastically when Hooper suddenly realised that Hawker had already created a neat solution to the BE.53's limitations. Its Sea Hawk fighter had been powered by a single Rolls-Royce Nene engine, but through the application of an ingenious engineering solution (patented by Hawker), the engine's exhaust had been bifurcated to emerge as separate flows either side of the aircraft's fuselage, thereby enabling the engine's thrust to be maintained instead of decreasing significantly through the employment of a more traditional long fuselage jet pipe to the tail. Hooper concluded that the same bifurcated exhaust arrangement could be incorporated into the BE.53 jet lift engine, so that the 'hot' end of the Orpheus exhaust was split into a second pair of exhaust nozzles. This would enable the engine to deliver all of its thrust either in the vertical or horizontal plane. Hooper and Fozard continued their work and established that further improvements could be made by redesigning the engine nozzles so that the simple bent vent pipes were replaced by a cascade of multiple vanes that turned the emerging air flow. There was also the question of gyroscopic effects that promised to be quite significant, but Fozard suggested that by counter-rotating the Olympus fan the gyroscopic effect would effectively be eliminated, thereby reducing any need for complicated stabilisation systems. Bristol was initially horrified by this proposal: it had adopted the Olympus turbine as a simple and cheap component, and claimed that the engine bearings would probably not be able to handle the loads, and that the cost of re-blading the Olympus component would be prohibitive. But eventually, it was agreed that the advantages of this arrangement outweighed the cost of its development and the combined improvements created the basis for what eventually became one of the most successful and revolutionary jet engines ever created – the Pegasus. These fundamental changes to the engine prompted Camm to state that the project should now have a 'proper military capability' that meant that, instead of being an unambitious liaison aircraft, the P.1127 could now be regarded as the basis of a true warplane.

The Ministry of Supply informed Hawker that there would be no financial support for the P.1127 project either (its interest in VTOL at that time being directed exclusively towards the Short SC.1) but Camm and Hooper revisited the offices of the MWDP in 1958 and quickly learned that American money would be available to fund the P.1127 project. Bill Chapman was encouraged by the Hawker design, although he felt that NATO would require something that provided almost double the projected radius of action proposed for P.1127. This led to more engine design work and the introduction of a water injection system that would boost the engine's take-off thrust and thereby almost double the amount of fuel that could be carried (changes and improvements to the engine design gradually increased deliverable thrust and the need for water injection subsequently diminished). In response to this encouraging news, a revised design was issued (the P.1127B), taking into account the drastically revised engine configuration that had been changed still further by the introduction of a new two-stage transonic compressor fan. This fan acted as a 'supercharger' on the original high-pressure compressor,

This rare image of XP831 illustrates changes to the aircraft during early trials. Outrigger wheel fairings are not fitted, and the tail RCV exhaust shroud is removed. Clearly visible is the fully inflated starboard air intake bag shroud. (*Aeroplane*)

creating what was in effect a 'high bypass' fan engine in which the bypass airflow emerged through the front 'cold' nozzles. The new P.1127 design was very different to the original proposal, and its proportions changed still further when the considerable bulk of the redesigned engine was taken into account. This necessitated a completely different undercarriage layout, with tandem main wheels and small outrigger wheels at the aircraft's wing tips. In order to minimise the length of these outriggers, the wing design incorporated significant anhedral, while still enabling the wing to remain intact as a one-piece structure running continuously across the aircraft's upper fuselage and engine (the entire wing section would be lifted out in order to access the engine). In forward flight, the aircraft was to be controlled by conventional ailerons, elevators and a rudder, but in a hover or vertical flight, the aircraft's control surfaces (with no airflow over them) would be useless. Control would be achieved by applying small applications of jet exhaust at the aircraft's extremities through small control valves, providing sufficient thrust to stabilise the aircraft in all three axes. Eventually, a satisfactory reaction control valve (RCV) system was devised, incorporating a continuous bleed system feeding RCVs that vented downwards at the wing tips, nose and tail, with the fuselage RCVs also capable of rotation laterally in order to provide yaw control. Col Chapman and the MWDP liked Hawker's completed proposal and also agreed to Bristol's request that three quarters of the engine's development cost should be funded by MWDP, leaving Bristol to finance the remaining quarter. In stark contrast, British official support was still virtually non-existent, the Ministry of Supply almost grudgingly agreeing to the possible provision of some wind tunnel facilities but still refusing to sanction a research contract, chiefly because there was no perceived civil potential for the project. Without the interest and support of America, the project would never have survived.

XP831 is pictured at Dunsfold during early flight trials. Visible here are the sensor vanes on the large test boom attached to the aircraft's nose, and the venturi tube fixed to the port side of the nose section (a similar tube was attached to the starboard side). The compressor fan blades on the Pegasus engine are also particularly prominent, as is the combined speed brake and main undercarriage door under the centre fuselage. (*Aeroplane*)

XP836 was the second P.1127 to be completed, making its first flight on 7 July 1961. It was destroyed on 14 December of that year following a crash landing at Yeovilton, caused by the loss of an engine nozzle during low level flying. (*Aeroplane*)

The first hints of the Ministry of Supply's interest came in the form of wind tunnel facilities, which gradually encouraged direct liaison among Hawker, the RAE's chief scientific officer (structural research) and the head of the RAE's transonic wind tunnel department. The MWDP's interest in the project also continued, the USAF's technical adviser to NATO suggesting that NATO's plans to develop an advanced strike fighter (its NBMR-3 project) should be bypassed and replaced by a derivative of Hawker's P.1127. This combination of American interest and the glimmers of enthusiasm from Britain's Ministry of Supply was sufficient to finally capture the attention of both the Royal Air Force (RAF) and Royal Navy (RN), from where a draft requirement for both a VTOL fighter and a VTOL transport aircraft emerged. By January 1959, official interest had grown still further, the Hawker team being informed that the new Ministry of Aviation (MoA) was considering the procurement of two prototype aircraft. On 23 January, Sydney Camm met with the chief of the air staff (operational requirements) and learned (much to his surprise) that the RAF were willing to ignore Defence Minister Sandys' assertion that manned combat aircraft would no longer be necessary, and that it now seemed reasonable to embark on the design of an aircraft with that to replace the Hawker Hunter in the ground attack support role. It was believed that a development of the new P.1127 design would be an ideal candidate for this requirement. Just a week later, a draft RAF specification had been drawn up and was already being circulated around government departments.

With tangible support finally beginning to manifest itself within Britain's corridors of power, consideration had to be given to the MWDP from where so much support had first emerged (including financing of the all important engine). Indeed, without the American MWDP money to finance the

XP831 in the hands of test pilot Bill Bedford, as the aircraft begins carrier trials on board HMS *Ark Royal* during February 1963. (*Aeroplane*)

XP972 was the first in a second batch of four P.1127 prototypes, making its first flight on 5 April 1962. It was written off following a crash landing at Tangmere on 10 October, after suffering an engine bearing seizure during a test flight over Sussex. (*Aeroplane*)

engine's development, the project would probably have never started. NATO was undoubtedly keen to encourage co-operation between countries on aircraft projects, therefore MWDP (influenced by NATO requirements and thinking) would be very unlikely to support continued development of the P.1127 if Hawker was seen to be 'going it alone' on what would be seen as an all-British subject. Hawker was therefore encouraged to seek some form of co-operation with a European partner, but although the concept of a joint project clearly had some merit, Hawker did not want to run the risk of losing any commercial benefits of producing an exclusively British product. Mindful of the BE.53 engine that remained British (but largely funded by American money), Hawker was also only too aware of the relationship that was being forged between Rolls-Royce and Avions Marcel Dassault, with Rolls-Royce's diminutive RB.108 lift engine having been adopted for Dassault's VTOL adaptation of its trusty Mirage fighter (another project that ultimately came to nothing). The situation was complicated and confusing, not least because NATO's emerging requirement for a new strike fighter was almost as nebulous as the RAF's stated needs. It was unclear what aircraft NATO would eventually require and it was equally unclear how such an aircraft would be funded, even if NATO did finally decide upon a specific design. Consequently, Hawker took the brave decision to continue development of the P.1127 independently, having concluded that when both the RAF and NATO eventually established precisely what kind of aircraft they really did want, there was no guarantee that these two requirements would result in one design, and the P.1127 might well be incapable of meeting either one. Hawker therefore proposed to continue developing the P.1127 as a research and proof-of-concept vehicle. Without any external financial support, Hawker issued manufacturing drawings to its experimental department during March 1959 and, a month later, the first metal was cut. It is to Hawker's great credit that so much faith was placed in the project and that

XP980 was the first P.1127 to introduce streamlined wing tip fairings and revised tailplanes set at an anhedral angle. It is pictured approaching the hover over Dunsfold. (*Aeroplane*)

XP976 was the first P.1127 to operate with inflatable air intake bag lips. It made its first flight on 12 July 1962. Unlike its predecessors, a pitot boom was attached to the leading edge of the tail fin. (*Aeroplane*)

Pictured over Dunsfold's runway, XP980 was employed on a variety of ground handling trials, designed to establish undercarriage loading and steering performance. (*Aeroplane*)

Hawker Siddeley's board ultimately allowed the P.1127 to be funded at its own expense for two years, even though Sydney Camm was often far from enthusiastic about it. It was only as the project progressed that he became increasingly convinced that Hawker was backing a potentially revolutionary aeroplane.

Just a few weeks after the initial manufacturing process began, the RAF's draft GOR.345 requirement for a Hunter replacement was shown to the Hawker team. The general (but still rather vague) requirements for a new ground attack and fighter-reconnaissance aircraft suggested that GOR.345 had effectively been written around the P.1127 design. In fact, the operational requirement (OR) was surprisingly modest, and, in most respects, it simply represented a new Hunter with VTOL capability. Simultaneously, the MoA requested that Hawker prepare costings and a manufacturing programme for two prototype aircraft, and a draft Research Specification (ER.204D) was shown to the company. Perhaps not surprisingly, this indication of growing British official support for the P.1127 prompted NATO to re-energise its interest in the new aircraft and Hawker officials were invited to Paris with Bristol and MoA representatives, in order to discuss the possibility of meeting NATO's requirement for a new strike fighter aircraft. However, it soon became clear that NATO's requirements had shifted quite considerably towards a much more sophisticated all-weather aircraft, and it was unlikely that the P.1127 could ever hope to meet this kind of demanding specification. Thus, NATO's interest in the aircraft dwindled again, but Col Chapman's enthusiasm for the P.1127 remained as strong as ever and, in the absence of any great NATO interest, he quickly fostered relations between Hawker and representatives of the US aircraft industry, with a variety of officials making visits to Kingston in order to learn more about the emerging project. This new relationship was not one-sided, as both Ralph Hooper and Robert Marsh (head of projects at

XP894 was the last of the second batch of four P.1127 prototypes, making its first flight in October 1963. It was damaged in a forced landing at Thorney Island on 19 March 1965 but returned to flying with the RAE after being repaired. It was destroyed in a landing accident at RAE Bedford on 31 October 1975. (*Aeroplane*)

Hawker) visited NASA's facility at Langley Field and also explored the various VTOL designs that were being pursued by the Bell Aircraft Corporation. By this stage, Bell was developing a tilt-rotor design, a ducted-propeller aircraft and the X-14, a small and simple aircraft powered by a pair of Rolls-Royce Viper turbojets. Its VTOL ability was achieved through the employment of thrust deflectors fitted behind the engines that directed the exhaust gases downwards in order to obtain jet lift. With a system of reaction control jets, similar to that being created for the P.1127, the Hawker and Bell teams had plenty to talk about. Hawker's reception at Langley Field had been even warmer and NASA's John Stack offered to conduct a series of free-flight model testing on the P.1127 design, while it was subsequently agreed that NASA would also undertake transonic wind tunnel testing. This test programme resulted in a one-sixth scale replica of the P.1127 that was equipped with working jet nozzles fed by internal fans. Eventually, it was placed in NASA's huge 30ft x 60ft wind tunnel at Langley and a team of four controllers (each operating one variable) 'flew' a series of tests on the model, culminating in transition from jet-powered hovers to conventional flight. Further tests were conducted in NASA's transonic tunnel with a smaller metal model, and rolling take-off and landing tests were performed outdoors. Once again, it had been American support for the project that enabled P.1127 to progress, but on 21 October, Hawker finally received a contract from Britain's MoA for the continuing design work at Kingston.

A magnificent photograph of the first P.1127, pictured at Dunsfold during the initial series of tethered hover tests. At this stage the aircraft was devoid of serial numbers and national insignia, the only markings applied to the airframe being small black/white calibration markings on the forward and rear fuselage, and even smaller markers adjacent to the jet exhausts. Also visible are the many airflow tufts that have been temporarily fixed to the rear fuselage surfaces. (*Aeroplane*)

Chapter 2

Supersonic Sideline

A draft contract and funding was issued on 1 June 1960 for two machines – XP831 and XP836. As these were regarded as research aircraft, it was also deemed necessary to extend official endorsement of the aircraft's engine, clearing what became the Pegasus 2 for a maximum 15 hours of VTOL operation and some 20 hours of conventional flight. NATO's vestigial interest in both the engine and the P.1127 had by this stage encouraged Bristol to develop a Stage 2 version of the Pegasus that could deliver a thrust of almost 20,000lb. This would have been more suitable for NATO's ambitious requirements, although it also encouraged Rolls-Royce to increase its efforts to promote its fixed vertical lift jet engine concept, which it still believed offered greater flexibility in terms of both aircraft weight and overall performance. In February 1960, the MoA formally requested that Hawker should clarify the NATO situation once and for all and the company confirmed that, in its present form, neither the P.1127 nor its engine would be capable of meeting NATO's demands as they stood. However, it added that Bristol's Stage 2 engine might be more appropriate for its requirements if a suitable aircraft design emerged. In fact, Bristol had just informed Hawker that the existing BE.53 Pegasus (improved to BE.53/3 standard) would probably be capable of delivering just 10,000lb – half of the Stage 2 engine's expected thrust. Frustratingly, Hawker had anticipated that the prototype P.1127 would probably weigh in at 10,000lb, and this prompted Stanley Hooker to carefully revise his design estimates. Recent bench running of the Pegasus had produced 11,500lb thrust, and this promised to offer a margin of power for the prototype's initial hovering trials, but with additional power needed for the aircraft's reaction controls (fed by high pressure air bled from the engine), it was clear that the aircraft would be critically short of jet lift thrust. Further concern was raised when Hawker's Chief Experimental Test Pilot Hugh Merewether was involved in an accident whilst evaluating Bell's X-14 during April. After suffering gyroscopic coupling problems, the aircraft ran out of available lift power and landed heavily. This emphasised that the P.1127 would need a good reaction control system that had sufficient power to maintain hover stability in pitch, roll and yaw.

On 12 April, the MoA requested that Hawker should produce a tender for a further four prototypes. Meanwhile, on 3 May, the first Pegasus engine (No 905) was transported from Bristol to Kingston for installation in the first aircraft. Construction was advanced by this stage and the transonic wind tunnel tests (and free-flight model research) conducted by NASA had yielded useful results. Back in the UK, the aircraft's reaction control ducts and valves were tested at Gloster Aircraft's Brockworth factory while Martin-Baker aircraft continued work on the ejection seat that would be fitted. The first run of an installed engine took place on 31 August (although this was not flight-cleared) and an 11,300lb-thrust Pegasus 2 was installed on 13 October. Hawker accepted that these first engines would be life-limited and that the first tests would actually be only jet-borne hovers, so that a full investigation of the aircraft's control characteristics could be explored in relatively safely, just a few feet above the ground. In order to avoid problems with ground effects and the ingestion of exhaust gases, model tests of a projected grid pad were completed, and a full-scale concrete pit was constructed at Hawker's test airfield at Dunsfold in Surrey. The pit was some 88ft long, 40ft wide and 4ft deep, with cascades to deflect exhaust gas through a metal grid base and out through an upwards sloping ramp at the end of the pit. A Pegasus engine was installed on the test grid on 22 September for a trial run, after that it was returned to Filton for examination and refurbishment. Meanwhile, the first P.1127 (XP831) had been transported to Dunsfold for final assembly and system checks before being

A quartet of Hawker Kestrels pictured during a publicity photo shoot, staged shortly after the formation of the Tripartite evaluation squadron at RAF West Raynham. (*Aeroplane*)

officially 'rolled out' on 31 August. After the aircraft had been weighed, it was quickly assigned to ground engine runs in a specially designed silencing pen, and although these runs went smoothly, XP831 did briefly catch fire during one of the tests when oil leaked from one of the engine's rear nozzles. Further tests were then completed over the metal grid on 22 September and, with no problems to address, the go-ahead was finally given for the first tethered flight test. Suitably prepared for the start of the P.1127's test flight programme, Bill Bedford walked out to XP831 on Dunsfold's test grid pad on the morning of 21 October and, at long last, the VTOL concept finally began its translation into a viable aeroplane.

The first tethered 'flights' were performed with great care, as it was impossible to predict how the aircraft would react until it actually left the ground. Although XP831 rose only a matter of inches from its pad, the aircraft yawed, pitched and rolled in a seemingly alarming fashion, but once the aircraft's jet-borne handling had been established, these early hovers soon began to look more stable. Within a matter of weeks, the aircraft was declared safe to hover without tethers and attention then shifted

While the Kestrels were evaluated in Norfolk, the P.1127 test programme continued at Dunsfold. This photograph of XP980 shows the aircraft in a less-than-pristine condition during rough field tests. Despite the seemingly flimsy appearance of the aircraft's landing gear, it performed surprisingly well during tests, and no major changes to the undercarriage design were needed. (*Aeroplane*)

towards the aircraft's flight characteristics. Bill Bedford made the first conventional flight in XP831 from RAE Bedford on 13 March 1961 and, by the end of that month, the aircraft was ready to be flown back to Dunsfold, having completed eight more flights. Further testing from Dunsfold revealed some problems with longitudinal control, and less severe problems with directional control when the landing gear was extended. Conventional landings were hampered by excessive trim changes when the aircraft approached ground effect, and similar problems were caused by the deployment of flaps and airbrakes; however, most of these problems had been anticipated and modifications were already being prepared to rectify these deficits. Another significant issue was the effect of hot gas re-ingestion during hovering at heights below 50ft. This resulted in various changes to the aircraft's air intakes, including the use of larger bulbous lips for initial hover trials, designed to reduce exhaust re-ingestion. These were removed for the initial conventional flight trials and were eventually replaced by smaller lips when more engine power became available. Ultimately, the issue was resolved through the use of inflatable bag lips that could be deflated for forward flight.

The second P.1127 (XP836) arrived at Dunsfold during June and during the following months it began the expansion of the flight envelope, reaching a speed of Mach 1.2, an altitude of 40,000ft and a manoeuvring limit of 6g. Its contribution to the test programme was cut short in December 1961 when the aircraft's port 'cold' exhaust nozzle became detached during a high-speed run at low level. Test pilot Bill Bedford diverted to RNAS Yeovilton but, during final approach to the runway, the

XP831 performed a series of landings and launches from HMS *Ark Royal* during February 1963. By this stage, the Admiralty had embraced the P.1154 project and the deployment encouraged the Royal Navy to maintain its interest in the programme. Test Pilots Bill Bedford and Hugh Merewether operated the aircraft from the carrier for some six days and demonstrated that the aircraft was easier to operate from a carrier than a conventional aircraft. But despite this, the Navy soon turned its attention to the American F-4 Phantom. (*Aeroplane*)

Two superb air-to-air images of XP972 during its visit to the 1962 SBAC Farnborough show. Tragically, the aircraft remained active for only a few more weeks until 30 October, when Hugh Merewether was flying the aircraft on a low-level test over Hampshire at a speed of some 550kts. The aircraft's engine suddenly suffered a surge and bearing failure, resulting in a fire that forced Merewether to head for the nearest airfield, which was at Tangmere. On landing, the undercarriage failed, and a serious fire ensued. The aircraft was transported to Kingston for examination, but it was not repaired. (*Aeroplane*)

aircraft entered into an uncontrollable roll, prompting Bedford's ejection and the destruction of the aircraft after it struck a farm building. This mishap did not affect the programme and, three months later, the 13,500lb thrust Pegasus 3 was ground run, while the third prototype (XP792) made its first flight in April. The fourth prototype (XP796, first flown on 12 July) incorporated changes to the wing leading edge that were designed to improve handling, and testing progressed well until 30 October 1962, when another accident occurred. This time, it was an engine bearing failure that forced Hugh Merewether to make a forced landing at RAF Tangmere; the undercarriage collapsed, and the aircraft was extensively damaged by fire. A more significant event occurred on 16 June when XP831 crashed in front of a huge audience at the Paris Air Show. Ironically, the cause of the accident was relatively minor; a small piece of debris became lodged in the aircraft's engine nozzle actuation motor, which caused the nozzles to shift rearwards during a hover demonstration and jet lift was immediately lost resulting in a catastrophic fall. The cause was not a concern but the embarrassment of such a public incident was immeasurable. But even this accident did not slow progress; the P.1127 had been deployed on board HMS *Ark Royal*, in response to growing interest from the Royal Navy. XP831 performed well during these sea trials and the deployment ultimately paved the way for maritime versions of the aircraft that were to follow many years later. But these initial sea trials had a more immediate effect on the P.1127 programme, in that they indirectly led to the creation of the production warplane that was created from it – the Harrier.

While development of the P.1127 progressed, other significant events were unfolding. By now, NATO had formulated NBMR-3, calling for a supersonic strike and attack aircraft. With no clear indication of where the P.1127 project would lead, Hawker's designers inevitably turned their attention to NATO's requirement and looked at more radical developments of the P.1127 design. Ralph Hooper examined the possibility of creating a new version of the Pegasus engine with an ingenious Plenum Chamber Burning (PCB) system that would burn bypass air flowing into the engine's 'cold' exhausts. He estimated that it would enable an aircraft to achieve Mach 2.0 at 50,000ft, although (perhaps wisely) the concept was not broadcast too widely, in case it compromised interest in the existing P.1127 as a potentially less ambitious attack aircraft. Chapman was immediately enthused by the proposal when he visited Kingston, and he encouraged Hawker to proceed with the new design (P.1150). It eventually matured into a serious proposal that was in direct competition with other designs being offered by consortiums from Rolls-Royce and Sud Aviation, Fokker and Republic, and Breguet and Fiat. All three designs employed vertical lift engines, and, in order to meet the 'international' nature of the NATO competition, Hawker was encouraged to enter into a joint design proposal with a German consortium, which eventually resulted in the P.1150 design being modified to incorporate two fixed vertical lift engines in addition to the main Bristol PCB BS.100. But with the vectored-thrust Pegasus having already demonstrated its potential, Hawker eventually reverted to a simpler design that employed only the BS.100 engine, and this was submitted to NATO for consideration as the P.1154. Given the demonstrable success of the P.1127, it was hardly surprising that Hawker's P.1150 was eventually declared the most promising proposal, but politics swiftly intervened and when France opted to proceed with its Mirage IV project regardless of NATO's wishes, the NBMR-3 project was effectively dead. The result was utter confusion with NATO unsure of its future requirements, France increasingly entrenched in its own unilateral position, and Hawker left with a promising design that no longer had a customer. It was at this stage that British politicians stepped in and encouraged Hawker to look towards the possibility of creating a strike aircraft that would be suitable for both Fleet Air Arm (FAA) and RAF service. The Royal Navy was already looking for a new supersonic interceptor and, although the RAF was looking towards TSR2 as its new tactical strike platform, there was an obvious possibility of creating an aircraft that would exceed the requirements that had been laid out in GOR.345.

Possibly the only occasion where three P.1127 prototypes flew together, XP831, XP976 and XP980 are pictured over southern England in the hands of test pilots Bill Bedford, Hugh Merewether and Duncan Simpson. As can be seen, all three aircraft show variations in their external modification states, with differing tailplane positions, wing layout and engine exhaust fairings. (*Aeroplane*)

Above: A misty morning at RAF West Raynham, with seven Hawker Kestrels on the Central Fighter Establishment's (CFE) apron, ready for another day of evaluation flying. (*Aeroplane*)

Below and opposite: After initial trials at West Raynham, the Kestrels were deployed to the former RAF airfield at Bircham Newton, where pilots from the UK, US and Germany evaluated the aircraft's take-off and landing performance in various conditions, ranging from short runways and semi-prepared surfaces, through to grass strips and temporary metal landing areas. (*Aeroplane*)

Hawker created a new proposal for the P.1154 suited to the requirements of both the FAA and RAF; the land-based variant as a single-seat machine with terrain following radar, while the naval version would include a second seat for an observer and would be armed with advanced air-to-air missiles. There were clearly some roles that would be applicable to both variants but, from the outset, it seemed unlikely that a single design could adequately meet the needs of both services. More importantly, both the RAF and FAA were undoubtedly more concerned with other projects. The RAF was keenly pursuing the hugely advanced TSR2 project, constantly embellishing the aircraft with more and more capabilities, while the Navy was looking across the Atlantic. During June 1961, an F-4 Phantom visited RNAS Yeovilton (as part of an appearance at the Paris Air Show), in order to enable Royal Navy officials to examine the aircraft in some detail. Although the P.1154 seemed like an attractive proposition, the FAA (driven by Lord Mountbatten) was eager to justify further spending on an ambitious aircraft carrier programme and the VTOL P.1154 was at odds with this position. Clearly, a VTOL aircraft did not necessarily require a fleet of huge aircraft carriers, whereas the conventional F-4 Phantom did. McDonnell's aircraft was a proven design, available at a competitive price, and it justified the Navy's requirement for further carrier spending. Almost inevitably, the P.1154 soon became the victim of inter-service squabbling, and despite a long and complicated developmental process, the project ultimately became unsustainable and hideously expensive. When a new Labour government came into power during October 1964, Defence Minister Denis Healey quickly put the matter to rest and cancelled the entire project. The Royal Navy was, of course, happy to accept Healey's alternative proposal to order a fleet of F-4 Phantoms, while the RAF was content to concentrate on TSR2, although this too was soon abandoned when the RAF accepted that the American F-111 would be a more affordable and practical proposition. However, Healey was not the 'axe murderer' often portrayed by military pundits. His primary motive was to equip the RAF and FAA with effective aircraft that could be afforded, and P.1154 showed every sign of becoming uncontrollably expensive. The aircraft had yet to be built and tested, and it seemed inevitable that countless issues would delay the development of such an advanced machine. Perhaps most significantly, nobody had seriously addressed the issues surrounding the effects of PCB engine exhaust on carrier decks, and of course, there were no guarantees that the advanced BS.100 engine would be developed within a reasonable time scale. But Healey did understand the viability of the VTOL concept and the potential of Hawker's P.1127. Consequently, despite cancelling P.1154, he redirected his full support towards the creation of a more modest ground attack aircraft based on the P.1127 design.

Thankfully, the RAF's interest in the P.1127 had not diminished while the abortive P.1154 programme unfolded, and in January 1960, the RAF's Central Fighter Establishment (CFE) had been instructed to investigate the viability of a developed P.1127 as a combat aircraft. This led to GOR.345, and when Bristol announced the development of the 15,000lb Pegasus 5 (which first flew in the final P.1127 XP984), it seemed clear to the RAF that a useful aircraft could be created. Efforts were made to secure collaborative interest in the aircraft (largely because of ongoing liaison with German manufacturers and the all-important financial support from America), and agreement was reached in 1962 to produce a new batch of nine P.1127s for operational evaluation by all three nations. On 16 January 1963, a Tripartite Agreement was signed between Britain, Germany and the US, with each nation eventually financing the development and operation of three aircraft. Manufacture of these aircraft was delayed until mid-1963 in order to incorporate the latest design developments, and ten pilots were selected to fly the aircraft. The British and German crews were regular RAF and Luftwaffe personnel, while America opted to nominate test pilots, chiefly because they regarded the project as a technical exercise, rather than an operational evaluation. The first aircraft (XS688) made its first flight on 7 March 1964, and although largely similar to the final aircraft in the first P.1127 batch, it featured a slightly longer fuselage to balance the aerodynamic thrust properties of the Pegasus 5 engine.

With airfield testing completed, the Kestrels were dispersed to locations in the field, using various sites within the Army's Stanford Training Area. Aircraft were housed within areas of woodland and operated from various clearings, either from the grass surface or from temporary metal pads that were set up for the exercises. Remarkably, the Kestrels proved to be extremely reliable, and no significant operating problems were encountered during these most rigorous tests. (*Aeroplane*)

The tailplane span was eventually enlarged to improve stability, and continual problems with the inflatable bag air intake lips prompted Hawker to abandon them in favour of a fixed lip. On 30 September, the refined design was named Kestrel FGA.Mk.1 and, by the end of the year, six aircraft were flying on initial testing and clearance trials. The first aircraft were delivered to RAF West Raynham (home of the CFE) in April 1965 and operational flying began immediately. Early evaluations were conducted directly from West Raynham, but activities then moved out into the surrounding countryside, including trials at a disused airfield at Bircham Newton, and remote clearings inside the Stanford Training Area near Thetford. These operations enabled the evaluation team to test the aircraft's VTOL capabilities on short runways, semi-prepared strips, and portable steel planking pads, although a variety of other surfaces were also tested, as was the aircraft's ability to operate as an attack aircraft and reconnaissance

Below and opposite: **Hawker Kestrel FGA.Mk.1 XS695 remained with Hawker after the Tripartite evaluation programme at West Raynham ended. With British national insignia restored, the aircraft appeared at the SBAC Farnborough show, carrying rocket pods on its wing pylons, and demonstrating the aircraft's remarkable VTOL performance. (*Aeroplane*)**

platform (the Kestrel was fitted with a nose-mounted camera). The evaluation was judged to be a great success and, much to everyone's surprise, the Kestrels operated reliably and effectively. In November 1965, the Tripartite squadron was disbanded, and six aircraft were transferred to the US, where they were employed on further test duties at Langley Field and Edwards AFB. The remaining pair (one other having been lost in an accident) rejoined the P.1127 trials programme.

The success of the Kestrel was a timely boost for both the RAF and Hawker, following the cancellation of P.1154. Almost immediately, the RAF shifted its attention back to the abandoned GOR.345 and, with the tacit support of Denis Healey, the Air Staff issued Requirement ASR.384 for a developed version of the P.1127, referred to as the P.1127(RAF). Although the new design was in effect a linear development of the Kestrel, it was in fact a very different machine, sharing a commonality of only 10 per cent. Fundamentally, the new aircraft had to meet more stringent performance figures in terms of load factors, fatigue limits, dive speed limits and much more. In order to meet these requirements (and those of the more powerful Pegasus 6 engine), the wing design was revised (chiefly through additional span beyond the outrigger wheel locations), the tailplanes were modified, and the air intakes were replaced by new variable geometry designs incorporating blow-in doors placed around the intake walls. The landing gear was beefed up, the RCV system was modified, and a water injection system was fitted to the new engine. New internal equipment included an inertial navigation system, a HUD (Head Up Display), a moving map display and a 70mm camera, with provision for a five-camera pod that could be carried under the aircraft's belly. This stores point was also stressed to carry ordnance and two weapons stations were also incorporated into each wing, capable of carrying bombs, rocket packs or fuel tanks. No internal guns were designed, but a bolt-on pod was designed to fit under each side of the lower fuselage, each one containing an Aden 30mm gun with ammunition. A fleet of six Development Batch aircraft was ordered in 1965 and the first of these (XV276) made its first flight on 31 August 1966. The DB aircraft were not destined for operational service and each aircraft was assigned to different aspects of the P.1127(RAF) test programme, based at Dunsfold, Boscombe Down and Filton. Experience with these aircraft soon demonstrated that the aircraft's revised air intake design was still unsatisfactory, and with the prospect of further increases in Pegasus engine thrust (and a resulting increase in higher mass flow requirements) seeming likely, Hawker's design team opted to redesign the intake yet again, increasing the number of blow-in doors to eight, and revising the outer fuselage contours behind the intake into a more streamlined shape. This was the only major change to the Development Batch airframe, and a contract for 60 production aircraft, designated Harrier GR.Mk.1 (GR signifying the Ground Attack and Reconnaissance roles) powered by the 19,000lb Pegasus 6 (Mark 101) was drafted in February 1966, with a go-ahead for production being given later that year before the contract was finalised early in 1967. A second contract followed to cover the two prototypes together with eight twin-seat dual-control variants, designated Harrier T.Mk.2. The first production Harrier (XV738) took to the air for the first time on 28 December 1967, flown by Duncan Simpson. The Harrier programme ran surprisingly smoothly, chiefly because most of the preliminary trials work was completed on the P.1127, and even though the Harrier was in effect a different aircraft, it retained virtually all of the P.1127's basic design features, enabling Hawker to 'leapfrog' many aspects of the Harrier programme. Indeed, much of the Harrier development work was concerned with refinement of the avionics and flight control systems. The Ferranti inertial navigation system was expected to be one of the more troublesome aspects of the programme, but it was quickly perfected to deliver a navigational accuracy of little more than a one mile error per hour of flight – something that was far better than anything achieved by other aircraft at that time. By August 1967, all six Harrier development aircraft were flying, and plans were made to improve the aircraft's performance even before it had settled into RAF service. The Pegasus 10 was rated at 20,500lb (thanks to better cooling of the engine's HP turbine blades and better water injection) and this (the Mk.102) was progressively retrofitted to the new aircraft that were then redesignated as Harrier GR.Mk.1A. Meanwhile, five Harriers were deployed to Boscombe Down so that service

Four Kestrels from the CFE's Tri-national evaluation squadron, pictured high over East Anglia early in 1965. Clearly visible are the fuselage aerodynamic strakes and the weapons pylons under each wing. (*Aeroplane*)

Kestrel XS694 tucked between the trees during dispersal trials in the Stanford Training Area near Thetford. (*Aeroplane*)

This stunning photograph of Kestrel XS688 shows the unusual tri-national insignia that became standard to all of the Kestrels assigned to the evaluation programme at West Raynham. XS688 was the first of just nine Kestrels that were manufactured. After the West Raynham trials ended, it was reallocated to Germany, but it was transferred to USAF control, and after further trials in the US, it was assigned to the USAF Museum. (*Aeroplane*)

evaluation of the aircraft could begin prior to achieving a CA release, while two more machines conducted trials from Dunsfold with a variety of external fuel tanks, bombs, SNEB-Matra rocket pods and other equipment.

Under the leadership of Duncan Simpson, the Harrier Conversion Team was set up in 1969, comprising four experienced Hunter pilots who had been selected by weight as much as by experience. As ever, the quest for an operational VSTOL aircraft was still being driven by a constant battle between power and weight. For some ten weeks, the team carefully studied all aspects of the Harrier's systems and learned as much as they could about the aircraft's aerodynamic properties from John Fozard. Their accumulated knowledge was then used as the basis for the HCT's Ground School syllabus with which the RAF's first Harrier pilots would be trained. The team's first hands-on flying took place at Chivenor, where the pilots completed a short refresher course on the Hunter before moving to Ternhill where they flew a six-hour course on Whirlwind helicopters, studying all aspects of VTOL flying. There then followed eight hours of flying on the Harrier itself. At this stage, there was still no dual-control variant of the aircraft available, and each pilot had to become accustomed to the Harrier's handling qualities through a combination of study, trial and error, although some very unusual type conversion training techniques were employed. Most of the initial solo flights were accompanied by Duncan Simpson in a Hunter, starting with a conventional flight that culminated in an equally conventional landing that (without jet lift) required the Harrier to touch down at some 160kts – this was probably the most difficult and dangerous of all types of Harrier landing. Subsequent flights introduced the pilots to VSTOL operations and included some very unorthodox conversion flying in a Dove (flown by Duncan Simpson), with the four pilots carefully studying the recommended approach and departure procedures over Dunsfold (talked through by Simpson) prior to practising transitions to and from jet-borne hovers in their Harriers. Finally, the pilots conducted a series of short take-offs and landings from both the runway and grass areas, and each made a vertical landing onto a small 50ft pad hidden in woodland near markers on adjacent trees acting as visual cues; the pilots had to land in the clearing virtually blind, making visual contact with the pad at little more that 15ft from touch down. The HCT then moved to RAF Wittering on 16 May, equipped only with its batch of single-seat Harriers, and a couple of twin-seat Hunter T7 chase aircraft and procedures trainers. A significant proportion of the initial training was exported back to the Kestrel's former home at West Raynham, where the concrete pads built for the TES trials were already in place and ideal for Harrier VTOL training. Despite the absence of a dual-control Harrier, the HCT's activities proceeded rapidly and smoothly, and by August 1970, the HCT was busy training the first instructors for the new Harrier Operational Conversion Unit (OCU). Two months later, the first Harrier T.Mk.2 was delivered and No 233 OCU was formed at Wittering, enabling the HCT to be wound down. The first operational Harrier squadron was one of the RAF's most famous – No 1 Squadron, which had previously been operating Hunters at West Raynham. Its first Harrier aircraft (XV476) was delivered to Wittering on 18 April 1969, with another three aircraft delivered to the unit during the same month. By July 1970, No 1 Squadron had its full complement of 18 aircraft (although this process had been slowed not by technical problems, but by occasional bird strike and ingestion problems – something that was to become a continual headache throughout the Harrier's service life) and re-equipment of the RAF's second unit (No 4 Squadron) then began. Its first aircraft (XV779) was joined by a further 14 aircraft by the end of the year and the unit established itself at Wildenrath, where RAF Germany's (RAFG) Harrier operations were to be concentrated. The second RAFG Harrier unit was No 20 Squadron, which began conversion late in 1970, and was followed by No 3 Squadron early in 1972, the RAFG force being declared fully operational in January of that same year. Wildenrath, despite being a huge and well-equipped station, proved to be

The nine Kestrels were withdrawn from use towards the end of 1965 and plans were made to allocate the aircraft to the three nations that had financed them. Germany expressed no further interest in the aircraft, and it was then proposed that all nine should be transferred to US control and, as a result, they were allocated Nos 64-18262 to 64-18270. However, three aircraft were then transferred to Hawker for further test duties, while the rest were shipped to the US for further evaluation by USAF, Army and USMC pilots. The aircraft was re-designated as the VZ-12 and then re-designated as the XV-6A. (Tim McLelland Collection)

a less-than-ideal location for the RAFG Harrier force, being some considerable distance from the East German border. Consequently, supporting the Army's activities (that were always inevitably some distance away) required a considerable amount of expensive and complex logistical backup that eventually encouraged the RAF to switch operations (during 1977) to the more suitable airfield at Gutersloh, which was vacated by the resident Lightning squadrons (their air defence role being assumed by Phantoms at Wildenrath). Gutersloh, just 75 miles from the border (and the RAF's most easterly 'Allied' airfield) then became RAFG's permanent Harrier base, comprising two enlarged squadrons after No 20 Squadron gave up its aircraft in order to re-equip with the (then) new Jaguar, and its relinquished Harriers were shared among the other two units. Thus, Nos 3 and 4 Squadrons became RAFG's core Harrier force, supported under wartime conditions by further aircraft from Wittering drawn from the OCU, flown by Qualified Flying Instructors (QFIs).

Two XV-6A Kestrels are pictured on board USS *Independence* during tri-service trials with the US Armed Forces. As can be seen, the aircraft were devoid of national insignia for these flights, with only 'Tri-service' titling applied in black on the aircraft tails. (*Aeroplane*)

XS688 as XV-6A 64-18262. It was transported to Dayton, Ohio, from Edwards AFB in 1970, becoming the first aircraft to be transported by C-5A Galaxy. (USAF)

Below and overleaf: In addition to evaluation by the US Armed Forces, two XV-6A Kestrels were also assigned to the National Aeronautics and Space Administration (NASA). Based at the Langley Research Center in Virginia, 520 (XS694) and 521 (XS689) were employed on test and evaluation duties for little more than a year. Aircraft 520 suffered a catastrophic landing accident on 27 August 1967 at Wallops Field. (Tim McLelland Collection)

Chapter 3

Combat Considerations

The concept of creating a Harrier trainer had been anticipated ever since the GOR.345 specification had emerged, although initial Harrier conversion training was achieved without a dual-control variant of the aircraft. Hawker's experience with the side-by-side seating arrangement designed for the Hunter trainer derivative seemed appropriate for the P.1127 but it was quickly realised that this would require a completely new nose section and possibly a new forward and centre fuselage too, leading to all manner of delays and difficulties that would be created by the need to accommodate the airflow demands of the huge engine air intakes. Consequently, there was no other option than to adopt a tandem seating arrangement that required only a minimal redesign of the Harrier's fuselage, and, by March 1960, Hawker had completed some preliminary drawings. It was not until February 1961 that the Air Ministry finally addressed the issue, but with the growing importance of the P.1154 (and continuing development of P.1127), another five years passed before a contract for a pair of twin-seaters was finally signed. Development of the Harrier T.Mk.2 then proceeded without any further delay, much of the development

Harrier GR.Mk.1 XV744 pictured just seconds before landing outside London St Pancras station during the 1969 Transatlantic Air Race. (Tim McLelland Collection)

A rare colour photograph of the first production Harrier GR.Mk.1 XV738, performing for the media at Dunsfold. The aircraft is unpainted and retains some panels painted in yellow primer, particularly the air intake area that was re-designed during the P.1127 Development Batch (DB) programme. (Simon Watson)

XV276 was the first of six pre-production P.1127 DB aircraft, making its first flight on 31 August 1966. It remained in use as a test aircraft until 1973, when it was destroyed in a crash at Dunsfold following an engine flame-out while hovering. (Tim McLelland Collection)

being shared by the ongoing single-seat P.1127 programme (particularly the weapons systems that would be common to both variants). The Air Staff specified that the trainer should retain as much commonality with the GR.Mk.1 as possible, and that, if necessary, it would be capable of being flown from the front cockpit as a single-seater with the same weapons carriage ability, so that it could be included in the RAF's overall total of available Harriers for combat operations.

The redesign of the Harrier was achieved with minimal alterations, although the result was an aircraft that looked markedly different to its single-seat counterpart. The cockpit and nose structure was shifted forward to enable a 47in plug to be inserted, providing space for a second cockpit. The cabin conditioning system (placed immediately behind the GR1's ejection seat) was modified to handle the larger twin cockpit demands and moved to the rear of the second seat. The position of the nose wheel bay necessitated the new rear cockpit frame to be moved aft where it was now directly over the bay, requiring the rear seat to be raised some 18in above the front seat. This coincidentally improved the rear seat occupant's view and was of great benefit to QFIs and Qualified Weapons Instructors (QWIs), affording them a clear view directly over the head of the student occupying the front seat. The centre of gravity considerations required the nose-mounted F95 camera and inertial platform to be moved to a new position under the rear cockpit and, to compensate for the extended nose profile, the rear fuselage (including the tail fin) was moved aft by some 33in and the fin structure was raised by 11in (and a revised ventral fin added) so that the aircraft's yaw stability could be maintained. By contrast, stability tests revealed that the tailplane position needed no changes and that the repositioned nose RCV (now some 56in further forward, combined with the input of the balancing rear RCV) did not require any significantly higher volumes of bleed air in order to maintain control. The wing and centre fuselage structure remained identical to the single-seater, and the only other noticeable design modification was the addition of vibration dampers in the tailplanes, necessary because of 'buzz' vibration caused during engine runs on the ground (the same harmonic problems were not created by the GR1). XW174 was duly completed as the first Harrier T.Mk.2 (essentially a development aircraft rather than a prototype) and it took to the air in the hands of Duncan Simpson on 22 April 1969. Sadly, the aircraft was destroyed only six weeks later when a fuel system fault occurred during a test flight and Simpson was forced to eject from the aircraft near Boscombe Down, sustaining severe injuries in the process. Development of the T.Mk.2 was not significantly delayed, however, as the second aircraft (XW175) made its first flight on 14 July and testing proceeded without any major difficulties. However, there was one significant problem that had not been foreseen. When the T.Mk.2 was flown at high angles of attack within a very specific speed range, the test pilots found that they were experiencing a rolling tendency caused by sideslip. Because most of the T.Mk.2 redesign had concentrated on the forward fuselage, it was believed that the cause of this directional instability was the redistributed airflow behind the cockpit breaking away, thereby reducing the fin's effectiveness. Further investigation revealed that this was not actually the case and that the problem was within the fin structure itself. Various redesign 'fixes' were investigated, starting with a simple (and moderately successful) 18in height extension to the fin tip, and flight testing suggested that an even greater extension would improve results still further, and so the fin's disproportionately tall structure grew even further (this time by 23in), although Hawker's structural stress experts were reluctant to advocate the modification and eventually the test pilots were asked to re-evaluate the shorter fin design. This they did and it was agreed that the 18in extension was in fact sufficient to cure the 'weathercock' stability problem. During test flying, it had been discovered that when the aircraft was exhibiting its undesirable instability, extending the ventral air brake tended to improve handling and so the design team linked its operating circuit to that of the tailplane. Subsequently (and on all production aircraft), when the control column is pulled hard (beyond normal cruise flight movements) to attain high angles of attack, the air brake automatically extends to 26 degrees, retracting when stick pressure is reduced.

Development Batch P.1127 XV279 pictured during trials at Dunfold, with test pilot Duncan Simpson entering the aircraft's cockpit. Like all but the last of the DB aircraft, XV279 featured an interim-standard air intake with six blow-in doors (production aircraft featured eight larger doors) and a separate fairing ahead of the forward exhaust nozzle. Wearing standard RAF camouflage, the nose cone is painted fluorescent orange, and the titles 'Hawker Siddeley Harrier' are applied in white and yellow. (*Aeroplane*)

XV280 was the penultimate aircraft in the batch of pre-production DB aircraft, manufactured for flight testing. Clearly visible are the six small air intake blow-in doors that were common to all DB aircraft, together with the forward jet nozzle fairing that stood proud of the fuselage side. In all other respects, the aircraft was essentially similar to the production-standard Harrier GR.Mk.1. (Simon Watson)

A batch of 12 Harrier T.Mk.2 aircraft was ordered in 1967 (later increased by an additional five airframes) and, after completion of flight testing and development (and attainment of a CA release), the first trainer aircraft was delivered to the Harrier OCU at Wittering in July 1970. Further deliveries were made to Wittering and Wildenrath, and by 1972, all of the Harrier squadrons had their own dual-control aircraft. As with the single-seater, the T.Mk.2 was also quickly retrofitted with a more powerful 20,000lb thrust Pegasus 102, and redesignated as the T.Mk.2A.

The Harrier's reduced wartime vulnerability was undoubtedly the aircraft's key asset but it was also clear that the Harrier would give the RAF an ability to provide a swifter response to Close Air Support tasking. TES recommendations were studied and refined over a period of four years and provided the basis for two basic concepts proposed for the Harrier force. Firstly, the Wittering-based aircraft belonging to No 1 Squadron were assigned to direct support of the ACE Mobile Force (Air) on the NATO flanks, as part of SACEUR's Strategic Reserve (Air). Secondly, the larger RAFG force would be assigned to No 2 ATAF. When No 1 Squadron formed, the unit quickly explored the Harrier's operational potential and its aircraft were deployed to various dispersed sites around the UK, as well as more distant locations in Norway and Cyprus. Operations from ships were also conducted (including a deployment to *Ark Royal*) and both Tromsø in Norway and Vandel in Denmark were soon allocated as the squadron's primary operational forward bases, with another seven bases later being added as designated wartime sites. Typical wartime sorties were expected to counter Warsaw Pact armoured vehicles that would probably be moving west through Finland's and Norway's mountain passes. In order to counter these targets, BL.755 cluster bombs and SNEB 68mm rockets (combined with the aircraft's semi-permanent

Harrier GR.Mk.1 XV758 performed a series of deck landing trials on board HMS *Blake* during August 1969, designed to demonstrate that the aircraft was capable of operating from small flight decks and also capable of operating independently of the usual wind-over-deck constraints that affect more conventional carrier aircraft. (Tim McLelland Collection)

Aden guns) were to be the Harrier pilot's weapons of choice. Typical sorties were expected to be of almost an hour in duration, extending to a radius of around 150nm (the aircraft carrying drop tanks for most missions). The Harrier's INAS and moving map display would provide the crews with essential navigational and attack information for every flight although target acquisition (and a great deal of the en route navigation) was to be performed visually, assisted by Forward Air Controllers (FACs) on the ground. Development of the Pegasus engine quickly resulted in a new Mk.103 version that delivered 21,500lb thrust (permitting an increase in all-up VTOL weight) and the Harrier GR.Mk.1A fleet was progressively refitted with this engine, being re-designated as Harrier GR.Mk.3 in the process. By 1975, the whole Harrier fleet (including the twin-seaters that were redesignated as the T.Mk.4) had been upgraded to this standard; as part of this process, the GR.Mk.3 airframes were gradually equipped with a fin and tail-mounted passive Radar Warning Receiver (RWR) and a new Laser Rangefinder and Marked Target Seeker (LRMTS) system, housed in a new nose fairing, giving the aircraft an unusual dolphin-esque appearance (the twin-seaters were also progressively upgraded to the same standard). This device produced a laser pulse that provided the pilot with target range and location data while also providing a search capability, seeking infrared radiation scattered from a target being illuminated by a

Below and overleaf spread: The Harrier first grabbed the media's attention in May 1969 when two aircraft (XV741 and XV744) were assigned to the *Daily Mail* Transatlantic Air Race, performing remarkable point-to-point flights between downtown Manhattan and London's St Pancras station. The Harrier had entered operational RAF service with No 1 Squadron just one month previously, and the two race aircraft were temporarily assigned to Boscombe Down for pre-race trials with the aircraft's bolt-on refuelling probe and extended 'ferry' wing tips. Although the refuelling probe became a standard piece of equipment for the Harrier, the wing tip extensions were not used operationally (they proved to be of little value). Perhaps not surprisingly, the RAF's Harriers won the air race although the FAA's supersonic Phantoms were credited with faster flight times. But the Harrier's unique ability to reach directly into the heart of London and New York (where the race start and end points were located) ensured that the RAF's team was victorious. (Tim McLelland Collection)

FAC on the ground. This enabled the FAC to designate a target by laser, so that the Harriers could deliver their weapons with extreme precision.

The enemy's defences were also taken into consideration and it was anticipated that mobile SA-6, SA-7 missiles would be the primary threat, together with mobile anti-aircraft artillery in the form of the ZSU-23/4. This would demand some very skilled evasion tactics from the Harrier pilots, and No 1 Squadron was soon well-versed in the art of low-level manoeuvring around the snow-covered fjords of Norway. The Harrier's new RWR system was an invaluable aid, providing the pilot with a cockpit display showing the direction and type of radar emission. In response to that the Harrier pilot would be obliged to take some very serious evasive action, aided by chaff and flare dispensers that were progressively fitted to the Harrier fleet. In addition to the risks of ground-based defences, the air threat was another important factor, and aircraft such as the MiG-21 *Fishbed* were expected to be a very significant problem for the Harrier force. However, the aircraft's small size, relatively light weight and excellent manoeuvrability (combined with the RWR, chaff and flares) suggested that in a combat environment, it would be more than capable of evading the attentions of marauding fighters. Maintaining a capacity to operate in this kind of hostile environment required No 1 Squadron to support continual deployments away from its home base at Wittering. During summer months, aircraft and crews would often deploy to Denmark (usually for a Tactical Evaluation exercise) and during winter months (usually in March), the squadron would deploy to Norway, where the unit's aircraft often appeared repainted in white 'Arctic' camouflage for the duration of each visit.

RAFG Harrier operations centred around a WARLOC (Wartime Locations) concept, with a combined fleet of around 36 available aircraft (plus a reinforcement reserve of 12 aircraft from the OCU). The Harrier force was to be deployed forward from its main base at Wildenrath to locations within the Army's No 1(BR) Corps area of responsibility. There were six pre-surveyed flying sites, two assigned to each squadron with capacity for up to eight aircraft at each location, together with a further six sites for 'step up' operations, a Forward Wing Operations Centre (FWOC) and a pair of logistics parks. At the main base (Wildenrath), the Harrier pilots had the relative luxury of a long, concrete runway and parallel taxiways from which to operate but, in the field, recovery would be made vertically, and departures achieved by short take-off. Many of these dispersed sites were selected strips of rural and urban roads that were built to 'schnellweg' standard (the equivalent of the UK's B-class network). Larger main roads and autobahns would have been even more suitable, but these would probably have been needed for emergency operation of less-versatile aircraft that required significant lengths of concrete from which to operate (and it was accepted that many roads would have to be kept free to be used as arterial convoy routes). Consequently, the Harrier sites were generally little more than small areas of clear road (or in some cases fields onto which pads and tracking could be laid), adjacent to forest camouflage cover – in essence the same sort of sites from which the TES Kestrel crews had operated many years previously.

The Kestrels that had been funded by America (now designated as the XV-6A) were re-evaluated as part of tri-service trials at Patuxent River and aircraft were deployed at sea on USS *Independence* and USS *Raleigh* in May 1966 – some weeks before Britain performed similar trials on HMS *Bulwark* with the P.1127(RAF). USAF and US Navy interest in the trials was again largely academic, but the USMC's interest was rather more serious. Tasked with the provision of air support for its ground forces, the USMC did not (and does not) possess its own aircraft carriers, therefore the concept of a STOVL ground support aircraft capable of operating more intimately with its ground forces was one that held considerable appeal. This interest eventually led to a rather unusual occurrence at the 1968 SBAC Show at Farnborough when, with almost no prior warning, Col Tom Miller (later to become Chief of Staff – Air for the USMC) and Lt Col Bud Baker, presented themselves to the Hawker Siddeley chalet and announced that they were in England to fly the Harrier, and would like to study the Pilot's Notes. Somewhat surprised, Hawker's team warmly welcomed the two pilots and, just a couple of weeks later, they were at Dunsfold flying Harrier development aircraft. They were both greatly impressed with the Harrier's abilities, and they returned to the US to give a favourable report to USMC and USN staff. By January, a USN team was in Britain conducting an evaluation of the aircraft and their findings led to funding approval (by June 1969) for a batch of 12 Harriers as part of a wider plan to acquire 114 aircraft for the USMC. It was also agreed that following the completion of the first 12 machines, the subsequent

Unlike the DB P.1127 aircraft, the Harrier GR.Mk.1 (and XV281 – the last of the DB aircraft) featured a revised air intake configuration with additional (and larger) blow-in doors, and a re-shaped fairing ahead of the forward jet nozzle, which was faired into the contours of the fuselage. This became the standard arrangement for production-standard Harriers. (Tim McLelland Collection)

No 1 Squadron was the first RAF Harrier squadron, receiving its first aircraft (XV476) on 18 April 1969. This Harrier GR1 proudly wears the markings of that unit and appears to have enjoyed the attention of a USAF SR-71 crew, who have applied their own additions to the more standard unit marking on the aircraft's nose. (Steve Bond)

aircraft would be manufactured in the US (under a licence agreement from Hawker Siddeley). This eventually led to a 15-year agreement with McDonnell Douglas for the manufacture and sale of the Harrier in the US, and also for the mutual exchange of design and development work conducted on Harrier developments during the same period (a similar arrangement for manufacture of the Pegasus engine was also set up between Rolls-Royce, Bristol and Pratt & Whitney). However, the costs of setting up Harrier production in the US were judged to be uneconomic and the subsequent aircraft were therefore manufactured in the UK.

As stipulated, changes to the USMC's Harriers were indeed minimal. Apart from the installation of an in-service naval radio fit instead of RAF-specific equipment, it was only the installation of a Sidewinder missile capability (on the outer wing pylons) that could have been regarded as a significant modification to the basic Harrier airframe. The Sidewinder capability was judged to be essential, as the USMC had deliberately foregone the opportunity to purchase an additional batch of F-4J Phantoms in order to fund the Harriers, and the Marines did not want to run any risk of the Harrier being perceived as an aircraft that could not defend itself. The 21,500lb Pegasus Mk.103 was chosen to power the aircraft but development of this engine derivative lagged behind the aircraft production process and so the first ten aircraft were fitted with Mk.102 engines before being re-engined at a later date. The only other change to the airframe was a weight-on-wheels switch to make safe all weapons once the aircraft was on the ground. Designated as the AV-8A, the aircraft were completed at Kingston, test flown at Dunsfold and then partially dismantled for transportation to St. Louis by C-5 or C-141. The first aircraft went to Patuxent River in

Harrier GR.Mk.1 aircraft from No 1 Squadron pictured during a dispersal exercise. The SNEB (Societe Nouvelle des Etablissements Edgar Brandt) 68mm projectile rocket pod (pictured on a loading trolley) became an important part of the Harrier's armoury, remaining in use until 1999. Also visible is the camera port fitted to the port side of the Harrier's nose cone, behind which a fixed F.96 camera was housed. (Tim McLelland Collection)

1971 for a US Navy Board of Inspection and Survey trial, making further short deployments to USS *Guadalcanal* and USS *Coronado*, before the AV-8A was officially approved for service use. From March 1971, the first batch of ten AV-8A aircraft was delivered to VMA-513 at Yuma in Arizona with further aircraft being delivered during the following year. Initial in-service experience was encouraging and only a few additional alterations to the aircraft were advised. The Ferranti 541 INAS was not popular with the Marines not only because of its relative complexity, but also the lengthy pre-take-off alignment time that compromised the USMC's rapid operational reaction ability. So, from the 60th aircraft onwards, the INAS was omitted, and a Smiths Weapons Aiming Computer was substituted – a system far less capable than the INAS but sufficient to provide necessary attack information, and free of alignment delays. The other major change was the removal of the Martin-Baker Mk.9 ejection seat, which was to be replaced by the Stencel SEU-3/A from the 90th aircraft onwards. The cost of these changes (plus others, such as the eventual removal of the ram air turbine) eventually necessitated a reduction in the overall AV-8A order to 110 aircraft. There was a real risk that Congress would cut the order still further before the final aircraft had been delivered, therefore the USMC deliberately delayed orders for a trainer derivative of the aircraft until FY (fiscal year) 1975. Eight trainer aircraft were eventually ordered, and these were manufactured in line with the AV-8A changes. The first TAV-8A aircraft were delivered to VMA(T)-203 at Cherry Point during the summer of 1976. Meanwhile, the AV-8A settled into USMC service without any difficulties and quickly proved itself as a versatile and increasingly valued part of the Marine Corps inventory. Although USMC operations were, in essence, very similar to those being conducted by the RAF in Europe (albeit with a much greater global mobility), the USMC did gradually devise its own operating techniques, and some of this experience eventually became adopted by British Harrier pilots, most notably the concept of 'viffing.' This unique ability was first discovered during the initial AV-8A trials at Patuxent River when Marine Corps Project Officer Maj Harry W. Blot was conducting his own hands-on evaluation of the aircraft. He declared himself greatly impressed by the Harrier and its ground support capabilities, but with fairly poor high-g manoeuvring (a symptom of the aircraft's small wing) and very poor rearwards visibility, he concluded that the aircraft was less-than-ideal as a fighter. Naturally, the Harrier was not designed for air-to-air combat, but the USMC did expect the aircraft to have at least some degree of self-defence ability. Blot had read reports about the possibility of shifting the Pegasus nozzles in conventional flight and the ways in which this vectored jet lift could theoretically be used to enhance the Harrier's manoeuvrability. He assumed that vectoring in forward flight (VIFF) had been explored by the RAF but, in fact, it had not. However, undeterred by the lack of technical advice on the matter, Blot got airborne in the first AV-8A and elected to try vectoring the aircraft's nozzles to their fullest extent – slamming them into fully-forward (reverse) thrust at 500kts:

> With pencil in hand, I slammed the nozzle lever into the braking stop position. The airplane started decelerating at an alarming rate, the magnitude of which I could not determine because my nose was pressed up against the gunsight. A terrible way to be, even in an imagined conflict. My movements were even further constrained by the fact that the violence of the manoeuvre had dislodged me from the seat, and I was now straddling the stick with my right hand extended backwards between my legs, trying to hold on for dear life.

NASA subsequently conducted a full VIFF test programme with an XV-6A Kestrel and a T-38 Talon during 1971, and air combat manoeuvring (ACM) trials were conducted by VMA-513 from Point Mugu. A second ACM trial (that included RAF personnel) was conducted at China Lake, and this led to a combined USMC/RAF trial that was conducted at RAF Valley, over a period of ten days. A Harrier (with strengthened nozzle drive and instrumentation) was flown against a non-viffing Harrier, a Phantom and a Hunter and, under all circumstances, the viffing Harrier emerged victorious. A second phase involved a Lightning F6 and also embraced a variety of ground attack profiles. Viffing was found to be of astounding value, and in theory at least, virtually no aircraft would be capable of positioning behind a Harrier if viffing was employed. Under most combat circumstances, it was impossible for the attacking aircraft not to fly through and overshoot. With further nozzle and engine modifications (enabling the nozzles to be vectored repeatedly for periods of up to 2½ minutes) the Harrier pilot could use the technique for a wide variety of defensive manoeuvres, prompting Blot to comment that 'the Harrier had crossed the line from being good to being great… its ACM capability is absolutely eye-watering'.

Starting in 1979, a total of 47 aircraft underwent conversion to AV-8C standard. ALR-45F/APR-43 radar warning receivers were fitted in the tail, wing tips and nose (this arrangement was preferred to the tail and fin-mounted system adopted by the RAF), and ALE-39 expendable munitions dispensers were fitted to the rear fuselage, together with an ALE-37 chaff dispenser, an onboard oxygen generation system and some lift improvement devices. The first of these aircraft entered service in 1983 and the AV-8C gradually supplemented the earlier variant with each USMC unit, although VMA-513 re-equipped exclusively with the C model. The AV-8A/C fleet remained in USMC service until the end in 1987, at which stage the USMC switched to the second-generation Harrier. However, this transition was not the end of the AV-8A's story. Spain had maintained an interest in the Harrier since 1972, but political relations with Britain were poor. Despite this, Hawker arranged for the Harrier to be demonstrated aboard Spain's SNS *Dedalo* (former USS *Cabot*).

Harrier GR.Mk.1 in a camouflaged 'hide' during a dispersal exercise. The aircraft wears the markings of No 233 OCU, the Harrier OCU. (*Aeroplane*)

No 4 Squadron was equipped with the Harrier from August 1970, the first aircraft to join the unit being XV779, and by the end of the year, a full unit strength of 15 Harrier GR.Mk.1s had been achieved. XV809 is seen at Wildenrath with 330gal ferry tanks in preparation for deployment to Armament Practice Camp at Cyprus during December 1972. (Pete Mears)

Most of the RAF's Harriers were delivered in a glossy camouflage finish, complete with full colour national insignia. However, within a few months the RAF adopted 'toned-down' national insignia, with all white portions removed. At a later stage, the gloss paint finish was replaced with a matt finish, as part of efforts to reduce the aircraft's visibility still further. (via John Adams)

Above and opposite: Images of No 4 Squadron's Harriers during dispersal exercises in Germany. Deployments away from the unit's home base at Wildenrath (and then Gutersloh) were a regular part of Harrier operations, ensuring that the Harrier force was able to relocate swiftly and effectively, ready to respond to any wartime requirement. (Colin Mears)

In typical political fashion, Spain refused permission for the Harrier to overfly Spanish territory, but the Navy sailed the *Dedalo* to a point off the Portugal coast. Test pilot John Farley flew a Harrier GR3 to the carrier non-stop and proceeded to demonstrate the aircraft's unique abilities. Thankfully, the fears that the vessel's wooden deck would burst into flames were proved unfounded and apart from a few scorch marks, the visit was completed to everyone's satisfaction. In order to expedite a Spanish order (and to avoid tedious political manoeuvrings), six AV-8A aircraft were simply added to the overall USMC order (Nos 159557 to 159562), followed by a pair of dual-control TAV8-A airframes. These were then resold to Spain as the VA.1 Matador (designated as the AV-8S by the USMC and Harrier Mk.54 by Hawker, the twin-seat aircraft being the Mk.59 or TAV-8S). When relations between Britain and Spain improved, a further order for five aircraft (161174 to 161178) was placed in August 1977, and these were purchased directly from Hawker Siddeley, designated as the Mk.55. Outwardly identical to the AV-8A, the Spanish Harriers differed only in radio equipment and the eventual fitment of Sky Guardian RWR equipment. By 1989, the AV-8S was reaching the end of its operational career and the Armada Espanola had, by this stage, transitioned to the second-generation Harrier. However, interest in the AV-8A was expressed by Thailand and a deal was signed for seven of the surviving AV-8S (and two TAV-8S) aircraft to be sold on to Thailand in September 1997. Refurbished by CASA prior to delivery, the aircraft (still retaining their Spanish paint schemes but with Thai insignia) were assigned to the HTMS *Chakri Naruebet*, officially referred to as the OPHC-911 (Offshore Patrol Helicopter Carrier). During periods when the aircraft were not at sea, the Harriers (assigned to No 301 Squadron) operated from U-Tapao as part of No 3 Wing of the Thai Navy. Initial flying training was undertaken in the US, with conversion to the Harrier taking place at Rota. Thailand's AV-8S were the last surviving operational examples of the original Harrier Mk.1/AV-8A series, but sufficient funding for training and spare parts was never properly secured and the aircraft were operated only sporadically until the few remaining examples were withdrawn in 2014.

Wintry scene at Bardufoss as a Harrier GR.Mk.1 from No 1 Squadron prepares to embark on a mission. No 1 Squadron regularly deployed to Norway as part of its training for wartime deployment, and Harriers were often seen wearing temporary 'snow' camouflage, with water-soluble white paint applied over the green portion of the aircraft's disruptive camouflage. (Tim McLelland Collection)

Introduction of the 20,000lb thrust Pegasus Mk.102 resulted in the Harrier fleet being upgraded to GR.MK.1A standard. This was succeeded by the Pegasus Mk.103 delivering 21,500lb thrust, and while this was incorporated into the USMC's AV-8A aircraft, it was retrofitted to RAF aircraft (and incorporated into new-build examples) together with new avionics, RWR gear, and a new LRMTS system housed in a revised nose cone shape. This created the Harrier GR.Mk.3. (*Aeroplane*)

Harrier GR.Mk.3 pictured on a minor German road during a dispersal exercise. The Mk.3's LRMTS nose cone is clearly visible, as is the laser seeker head, which is covered. Also visible on the aircraft's tail fin, is the forward sensor for the aircraft's RWR – the rear sensor being attached to the tip of the tail boom. (*Aeroplane*)

HarDet (Harrier Detachment) Belize was established during 1975 in response to security risks coming from neighbouring Guatemala. Six Harriers were sent to Belize International Airport during November, and Harriers remained deployed at the site until July 1993, the detachment becoming No 1417 Flight during April 1980. The unit applied its own markings in the shape of a crayfish emblem, applied to the aircraft's nose. (*Aeroplane*)

British naval interest in the Harrier had first developed with the abortive P.1154, but when the British government cancelled the CVA-1 carrier programme (and determined that all naval fixed-with forces would be withdrawn by 1972) the Navy had to drastically re-appraise its situation. It was assumed that the RAF would undertake future maritime missions and No 1 Squadron was cleared for ship deployment early in 1971, even though it did not take too long to accept that sustained operations at sea would not be possible. No 1 Squadron was assigned to wartime deployment in Norway, and it could hardly be in two places at once. Likewise, the squadron had no capability to operate in the air defence role and it was obvious that a dedicated maritime Harrier force was the only practical solution to Britain's needs. The Navy embraced what was first referred to as the Maritime Support Harrier (this was subsequently abbreviated to Maritime Harrier and then Sea Harrier). Exploration of the concept took place over many months and included a variety of potentially exciting options, including the use of a new 25,000lb Pegasus being developed by Rolls-Royce Bristol, and the employment of various weapons systems. But it was also obvious to the Navy that there was very little money available, and whatever the Sea Harrier was to be, it would have to be something relatively modest if it was ever to be financed, not least because there was also the fundamental issue of what ships the Harrier would operate from – and the considerable cost that these would incur. In fact, the ships appear to have been openly considered before the Harriers and it was during 1969 that the concept of a 'through-deck cruiser' was first proposed by the RN Ship Department at Bath. This vessel was to be assigned three main tasks, these being the deployment of anti-submarine helicopters, the command and control of naval and maritime air forces, and a 'contribution to air defence.' This latter category was vague, but it seems likely that this was the first indirect reference to the notion of re-introducing fixed-wing air power into the Navy. The RAF disputed the Navy's claims that any new aircraft carriers were needed or that an aircraft was needed for 'defence of the fleet.' Indeed, it asked (with tongues firmly in cheeks) what fleet was to be protected, and precisely how much defence could be achieved with maybe only a dozen Harriers. More to the point, as far as the RAF was concerned the introduction of Sea Harriers might convince politicians that the Navy was somehow capable of defending itself, and this might lead to a reduction in orders for its air defence variant of the MRCA (Tornado). But the Sea Harrier concept persisted and it was agreed that the Royal Navy could pursue a Naval Staff Target for a minimum-change version of the existing Harrier, redesigned to achieve air defence ability over a range of up to 400nm at altitude, reconnaissance ability over an area of 20,000 square miles within one hour at low level, and a strike and ground attack capability with a radius of action extending to 250nm. In effect, this specification outlined a truly multi-role aircraft albeit with a fairly modest capability, but one that could be successfully operated from a through-deck cruiser. Changes to the Harrier airframe were divided between those that were necessary to meet these specified demands and those that were required for operation to and from a carrier. For the former category, the weapons system was revised to incorporate a Smiths HUD driven by digital computer, combining air-to-air and air-to-surface weapon aiming capacity. Also included was a self-aligning attitude-reference platform, and, of course, radar, in the shape of Ferranti's Blue Fox that was developed from the Seaspray system used in the Lynx helicopter. Suitably modified for the air-to-air and air-to-surface requirements of the Harrier, it was also suitable for the hostile ECM environment in which the aircraft was expected to operate. Good though the new radar was, a plan to incorporate radar information into the HUD was dropped thanks to cost considerations, and the radar's display became a head-down TV screen inside the cockpit. The five weapons pylons were similar to those fitted to the RAF's Harrier GR.Mk.3 but with stronger release units. Compatibility with a wide range of weapons was incorporated from the start, including the Sidewinder (on outboard pylons), Martel and Harpoon. Perhaps most significantly, the Sea Harrier was afforded a Strike function and was cleared to carry the WE.177 nuclear store that gave the aircraft a destructive capability far beyond its more modest ground attack capacity. For carrier operations, other changes were incorporated, such as the removal of many magnesium components that would suffer from salt corrosion, and the incorporation of deck tie-downs (later fitted to RAF Harriers for operations in the Falklands). The other (and most obvious) change to the Harrier airframe was the redesign of the forward fuselage, necessitated by the new radar. The larger nose profile provided an opportunity to raise the cockpit and canopy so that it emerged beyond the height of the upper fuselage, thereby affording the pilot a greatly improved all-round vision that enhanced the Sea Harrier's potential as a fighter. This became a common feature in all subsequent Harrier developments.

During 1975, the Admiralty redesignated its new through-deck cruisers as 'Command Cruisers' in the shape of HMS *Ark Royal*, *Illustrious* and *Invincible*, each of which would ultimately accommodate six Sea Harriers. It was envisaged that two of these carriers might be deployed simultaneously, and an order for 31 aircraft was issued (the total order eventually rose to 57 aircraft) together with three development aircraft, designated Sea Harrier FRS.Mk.1. An initial contract for a design study was issued in 1972 but with issues such as a fuel crisis, the 'three-day week' and inflation, progress slowed

USMC AV-8A Harriers from VMA-542 and VMA-231 on board USS *Nassau*. The AV-8As were delivered in standard RAF camouflage with full colour US national insignia, although (like the RAF) the markings were quickly changed to low-visibility alternatives, which, in the case of the USMC, were black. (US Navy)

AV-8A 158975, proudly wearing the markings of VMA-513. This colour image reveals that the 'WF' tail code was applied in dark blue (rather than black), prior to the adoption of black low visibility national insignia and unit markings. (Mick Roth Collection)

AV-8A 159258 from VMA-542, complete with an AIM-9L Sidewinder training round under the port wing. (Jim Roth Collection)

until both customer and manufacturer began to accept that the order might never be placed at all. It was therefore something of a surprise to both Hawker Siddeley and the Navy when Defence Minister Roy Mason finally announced the Sea Harrier order in 1975 (indeed John Fozard only learned of the order via BBC News). The first development aircraft to be completed was XZ439 and this aircraft took to the air on 20 August 1978 in the hands of John Farley. Before the Sea Harrier was manufactured, trials with a Harrier GR.Mk.3 were flown with the Martel ASM with a balancing store on the other wing. These tests demonstrated that the Harrier could hover and land vertically in this configuration (a fairly heavy store for the diminutive Harrier) and test pilot John Farley successfully fired a Martel round to demonstrate that the missile's exhaust plume did not affect the performance of the Pegasus engine. Martel was swiftly replaced by the more advanced Sea Eagle ASM, and this missile became one of Sea Harrier's primary weapons. On 26 March 1979, HMS *Invincible* commenced sea trials and, on 18 September, the first Sea Harrier unit – No 700A Naval Air Squadron – was commissioned at RNAS Yeovilton in Somerset, having taken delivery of Sea Harrier XZ451. This unit eventually operated the first five production Sea Harriers and, after completing its role as the Intensive Flying Trials Unit, it became No 899 NAS – the Navy's shore-based training unit. The three operational squadrons (800, 801 and 802) followed on as production of more Sea Harriers was completed. Oddly, no twin-seat derivative of the Sea Harrier was ordered, the Navy having concluded that specialist training for STOVL deck operations was not necessary. Conversion training to the Harrier was undertaken by the RAF's OCU at Wittering and one of this unit's Harrier T.Mk.4As (XZ455) was funded by the Navy as part of this arrangement. However, a handful of former RAF Harrier T.Mk.4s were eventually transferred to 899 NAS at Yeovilton and redesignated as the Harrier T.Mk.4N with three new-build aircraft subsequently delivered directly to the Navy, enabling 899 NAS to eventually assume all naval conversion training on the type.

Lt Cdr Doug Taylor devised what became known as the 'Ski Jump', which enhanced the Sea Harrier's capabilities very significantly. By creating an upward curve to the end of a carrier's take-off area, he proposed that the Harrier could take advantage of an input of vertical velocity, effectively throwing the aircraft skywards. Not only would this enable the aircraft to take-off with heavier fuel or weapons loads, it would also enable deck sizes to be reduced and also impart greater flight safety on every take-off. For a normal short take-off (STO), the Harrier accelerates forwards at full power with the engine nozzles vectored aft. At the end of a carrier's deck, the nozzles would be rotated to 50 degrees and the aircraft would become airborne with a combination of jet lift and growing wing lift. With a suitable upwards-curved ramp, the aircraft could leave the deck at a lower speed (perhaps 60kts instead of 90kts) and with an automatic upwards velocity it would reach 200ft just a matter of seconds later, giving the pilot far more time to resolve any problems if there was an engine failure or other emergency. Likewise, normal STO departures from a flat surface must take into account the risk of a pitching deck that might be at the downward part of its cycle at the critical point of take-off. By 1977, a test rig had been constructed at RAE Bedford and the first Harrier take-off was performed successfully from the ramp on 5 August. The 6-degree ramp angle was then raised to 12 degrees by December and Harriers were able to demonstrate launches at speeds that were as low as 75kts, some 65kts less than a more typical STO. More than 1,000 ramp launches were performed, and the ramp angle was tested at a variety of angles, eventually reaching 20 degrees, at which the Harrier's undercarriage oleos were reaching their maximum compression under a 4g load as they went up the ramp. Unfortunately, both HMS *Invincible* and HMS *Illustrious* had already been completed with Sea Dart SAM positions on their bow structure and this restricted the incorporation of ramps to only 7 degrees. In comparison, *Ark Royal* was completed with a 12-degree ramp and HMS *Hermes* (which was still in service and adapted to handle Harriers) was fitted with a similar 12 degree facility.

One former USMC AV-8A was assigned to NASA and was employed on VSTOL research duties at the Langley Research Center. Apart from the radical change of colour scheme, it remained unchanged from USMC standard. (Mick Roth Collection)

AV-8A 158703 was employed on flight test duties at Patuxent River NAS, and received a liberal application of high-visibility orange markings during its time there. The aircraft crashed on 26 June 1981 while its pilot (who was killed in the accident) was making a demonstration flyby. The cause of the crash was attributed to pilot error. (Mick Roth Collection)

Chapter 4

Maritime Manoeuvrings

Initial operational capability on the Sea Harrier was achieved early in 1982, but as the crisis in the South Atlantic unfolded, the creation of a task force quickly emerged. It was obvious that the very core of this force would be carrier power and, therefore, the Sea Harrier, as this was the only combat aircraft that Britain could practically deploy in the South Atlantic. Of course, the Sea Harrier was designed to counter Soviet bombers or carrier-born Yak-38s, and nobody imagined that the Sea Harrier would ever be expected to fight Mirages. However, the assembled task force set sail with every available Sea Harrier (24 aircraft) embarked on board HMS *Hermes* and *Invincible*. History records that both the RAF's Harriers and the Navy's Sea Harriers achieved great success in the weeks that followed. It is true that the Argentine pilots were obliged to operate their aircraft at the very limits of their fuel endurance, which prevented them from engaging in any significant air combat over the Falklands, but it is equally true that the skill and professionalism of the British pilots was a deciding factor in Britain's victory. Various last-minute upgrades were made to the Sea Harrier. For example, the all-important AIM-9L Sidewinder was not even cleared for Sea Harrier use at the beginning of April 1982 and an emergency programme provided clearance in just a matter of days. Likewise, the aircraft's chaff and flare dispensers were not fitted at the start of the deployment south and they had to be dropped by parachute for fitment en route. But despite so many shortcomings and disadvantages, the Sea Harriers enabled crews to achieve the downing of 22 enemy aircraft (plus a helicopter) at the expense of only two losses, both of which were due to ground fire. Only four more aircraft were lost due to other accidents. The Falklands Crisis clearly demonstrated the value of carrier power and the versatility of the diminutive, unsophisticated but disproportionately potent Sea Harrier.

Post-Falklands, it had been envisaged that a re-winged Sea Harrier design would eventually be procured for the Navy, but when a similar plan being pursued by the RAF was dropped in 1980, it seemed clear that the Sea Harrier's development would have to be more modest. Most importantly, the sinking of HMS *Sheffield* and the *Atlantic Conveyor* had demonstrated that a look-down radar capability was essential and that both aircraft and sea-skimming missile detection would be a priority. It was also evident that the AIM-9L missile (and the 30mm cannon) required Sea Harrier pilots to manoeuvre at close range if they were to successfully acquire a target and, of course, the aircraft was not designed to be an agile dogfighter. The Harrier's unique viffing ability was certainly an asset but vectoring the aircraft's thrust inevitably resulted in a significant loss of energy and, although it gave pilots a formidable self-defence capability, it was only of limited use in terms of pressing home an attack. Thankfully for Britain, the Argentine pilots had been equipped with aircraft that were relatively old and did not have the advantage of a good Beyond Visual Range (BVR) radar and missile capacity, and which they were obliged to operate at distances that used every drop of available fuel. Clearly, this balance of capabilities could not be relied upon for every conceivable future conflict. A Mid-Life Update (MLU) programme was therefore embarked upon and, in the meantime, a more immediate Phase One update was initiated, for completion in 1987. This gave the Sea Harrier some important improvements, most notably the incorporation of twin Sidewinder launch rails, thereby doubling the aircraft's missile capacity. A new 'nozzle inching' facility was introduced (enabling the pilot to trim the engine nozzle position by a further 10 degrees to provide additional deceleration), and a new Microwave Aircraft Digital Guidance Equipment (MADGE) system was installed, roughly equivalent to the more common Instrument Landing System (ILS) fitted to many combat aircraft, enabling the Sea

Harrier to recover in poor weather without a talk-down facility. Development of the Sea Eagle missile had continued, and it finally entered service in 1987, providing the Sea Harrier with an outstanding 'fire and forget' system that could be employed against surface targets at long range. More Sea Harrier FRS.Mk.1 aircraft were ordered largely to replace those that had been lost (a total of 17 by this stage), but the Sea Harrier's MLU Phase Two programme was intentionally more ambitious.

During February 1985, British Aerospace (BAe) and Marconi received a project definition contract for the upgrade of 30 aircraft as part of a Sea Harrier Improvement Programme (SHIP). At the core of this project was new radar – the Ferranti Blue Vixen, and the Hughes (subsequently Raytheon)

HMS *Invincible* pictured during the 1982 Falklands Conflict. A Sea Harrier FRS.Mk.1 is prepared for launch while a second aircraft is seen leaving the carrier's 'ski jump' ramp at the start of a combat air patrol mission over the South Atlantic. (Terry Panopalis Collection)

Harrier T.Mk.8 ZB603 making a short landing at Wittering, during a training deployment from its home base at Yeovilton. The Navy's all-black paint scheme was derived from what was a common paint finish for RAF trainer aircraft, although the high-visibility black finish contrasted with the national insignia that were still applied in low-visibility colours. (Tom Cheney)

Harrier T.Mk.2 at Wittering with a single-seat Harrier GR.Mk.3 in the distance. The yellow patches on the trainer aircraft appear to be replacement panels attached during maintenance, awaiting repainting. (Tim McLelland)

AIM-120 Advanced Medium Range Air to Air Missile (AMRAM). The new pulse-Doppler radar was regarded as ideal for look-down capability and work on a production system was advanced by the time that an order was placed in December 1988 for the conversion of 29 FRS.Mk.1 aircraft to the new FRS.Mk.2 standard (four more conversions were ordered in 1995 together with a batch of 18 new-build aircraft). With the new radar (designed with a high degree of automation) and the 'fire and forget' AIM-20, the new Sea Harrier also incorporated a longer fuselage, courtesy of a 35cm plug that provided extra space to house the radar's processor and other avionics equipment. The radar also required the aircraft's nose profile to be revised again, and this time a more bulbous nose cone was simply grafted onto the existing forward fuselage. The design of the aircraft's wing leading edge was changed in order to improve handling, with a new kinked shape, deletion of one of the vortex generators and an additional wing fence. Other improvements were also proposed (such as leading edge wing root extensions and additional missile capability) but the projected costs prevented these from proceeding. The only other significant change made to the FRS.Mk.2 was the incorporation of a slightly more powerful Pegasus Mk.106 engine with improved thrust at lower operating temperatures. The first completed FRS.Mk.2 (ZA195) made its first flight from Dunsfold on 19 September 1988 in the hands of test pilot Heinz Frick. The second prototype (XZ439) was shipped to the US on board a new *Atlantic Conveyor* in January 1993, and was used to conduct live firings of the AIM-20 missile against target drones at Eglin AFB in Florida.

Sea Harriers from Nos 800 and 899 NAS pictured on board HMS *Invincible* shortly after joining the ranks of the FAA. Both aircraft are devoid of armament, with lower fuselage strakes replacing the Aden cannon pods that would otherwise be fitted in these positions. External fuel tanks are carried on the inner wing weapons pylons. (Tim McLelland Collection)

This striking image of the Sea Harrier FRS.Mk.1 illustrates the graceful lines of the 'navalised' Harrier design, with a revised nose section incorporating a raised cockpit position and a streamlined nose cone containing radar. (Tim McLelland Collection)

Sea Harrier FRS.Mk.1 XZ454 pictured shortly after delivery to the FAA, pristine in Dark Sea Grey and White colours, with the full-colour unit markings of No 800 NAS. (Royal Navy)

After an official handing-over ceremony at Dunsfold on 2 April 1993, the first aircraft was delivered to 899 NAS at Yeovilton in the shape of ZA176 during September 1993. With the Kingston factory now gone, these aircraft were manufactured at BAe's Brough factory, before being dismantled and transported to Dunsfold for final assembly and test flying. Although new build, the aircraft were fitted with Pegasus Mk.103s taken from redundant RAF Harriers before eventually being refurbished and modified to Mk.106 standard. In May 1994, the FRS.Mk.2 designation was changed to Sea Harrier FA.Mk.2, reflecting the fact that the new aircraft no longer had a reconnaissance role, and because the strike capability had been abandoned (the WE.177 was withdrawn from Naval service in June 1992). No 801 NAS became the first operational unit to take delivery of the FA.Mk.2 (in October 1994) and the FRS.Mk.1 was withdrawn from use over a period of months until the last example (ZD581) left No 800 NAS on 17 March 1995. It was not until 24 December 1998 that the last production FA.Mk.2 (ZH813) was handed over to the FAA. This was the last of the 'first generation' Harriers to be completed and it also therefore earned itself the distinction of becoming the last all-British fighter to be manufactured – if the Sea Harrier could truly be described as a fighter in the traditional sense. In subsequent years, the Gulf Wars, Balkans operations and Sierra Leone conflicts all called upon the Navy's participation, and the Harrier (either in the form of the FA.Mk.2 or the joint RAF/RN GR. Mk.7/9) continued to play a significant part in the Navy's order of battle until 2010. The original intention was to retain the original Sea Harrier fleet in service until at least 2012 when the Navy was to acquire the all-new Lockheed Martin F-35 strike fighter, but as the projected delivery date for this complicated and expensive design slipped further and further away (and the likely cost grew ever higher), the government's thinking began to change. During 2002, the Ministry of Defence announced that the Sea Harrier was to be withdrawn from 2006. The decision was ostensibly taken on the basis that there would be 'difficulties' in upgrading the Sea Harrier's capabilities still further and that 'other capabilities' were now available (this referred to the Type 45 anti-air warfare destroyer rather than any other aircraft type). It seems obvious, however, that the decision to abandon the Sea Harrier was made purely on the basis of cost savings, as it was accepted that early withdrawal of the Sea Harrier would save £135m and that a further £230m could be saved by not implementing another engine upgrade for the fleet. On 28 March 2008, No 801 NAS performed a five-aircraft flypast over Yeovilton to mark the premature retirement of the Sea Harrier from British service, and on the following day, the remaining Sea Harriers were ferried to RAF Shawbury to be placed in storage.

The production and development agreement made between Hawker Siddeley and McDonnell Douglas as part of the AV-8A programme (and a similar arrangement between Rolls-Royce and Pratt & Whitney) included the potential for continued development of the Harrier design and, in 1972, a joint US and UK Advanced Harrier programme was initiated. This was based around continued development of the original Pegasus engine that had now been transformed into the 24,500lb Pegasus 15. With a larger fan blade diameter and differing intake requirements, the engine could not be incorporated into existing Harrier derivatives, and it was therefore only applicable to a significantly redesigned aircraft that would become a 'second-generation' Harrier design. On 12 April 1973, a project definition phase was approved, leading to a document that was issued in December, detailing the proposed design requirements. For the United States, this would form the basis of an aircraft with which to ultimately replace the existing fleet of AV-8As when they reached the end of their useful lives, and also to replace the A-4 Skyhawk. For Britain, the new aircraft would replace the RAF's Harrier Mk.1 derivatives and possibly provide the Royal Navy with an aircraft suitable for operation on its new Through-Deck Cruisers (this project having first emerged before Sea Harrier). The result was the AV-16, although it was initially designated as the AV-8C. At Kingston, some very basic studies were already being made for an aircraft that could take advantage of the Pegasus 15 and these were mostly created under the project designation HS.1184. The Air Staff was not particularly interested in these developments, as the more conventional Jaguar was now about to enter service, and the RAF believed that for the close air support mission, the existing Harrier fleet was perfectly adequate. The American designation (AV-16) clearly demonstrated McDonnell Douglas' intention to double the Harrier's effectiveness in terms of range and payload capability, and the proposed aircraft was a significant improvement over the first-generation aircraft. With a new fuselage, supercritical wing, PCB engine, new avionics and more weapons stations, the new design began to look remarkably like the abandoned P.1154 and, in just the same ways as that aircraft had been dumped, the British government eventually decided to abandon its interest in the AV-16 during 1975.

Captured perfectly on camera, a TAV-8A (159379) from VMAT-203. Of note is the white line applied to the forward 'cold' engine nozzle, presumably intended to provide an easy visual guide to the nozzle's angle. (Francesco Checuz)

A rather 'battle worn' TAV-8A, illustrating how repair of the aircraft's paint finish has resulted in a distinctly patchy appearance. USMC Harrier trainers usually carried no external stores other than fuel tanks. (Mick Roth Collection)

Without Britain's participation, America was also ultimately forced to accept that with an estimated cost of more than US$2bn, they could not afford to continue alone, and it too reluctantly abandoned AV-16.

Hawker Siddeley continued examining less ambitious ways to improve the Harrier. It was clear that one of the aircraft's main deficiencies was its relatively poor ability to defend itself, and that a bigger wing would provide more lift and thereby improve the aircraft's capabilities. A bigger wing would also enable more weapons hard points to be installed and it would create additional volume for fuel capacity. By 1977, Kingston had received a feasibility study contract for what was known as the Big Wing to be retrofitted to existing Harrier aircraft. With a new supercritical design, three weapons points per side, leading edge wing root extensions and new slotted flaps, the new wing would be combined with a new forward fuselage that repositioned the cockpit higher on the fuselage. Additionally, improvements were made to the exhaust flow pressure recovery achievable under the fuselage, by fitting larger strakes (or gun pods) and a retractable cross dam device that served to create lift from the mutual cross flow of the four nozzle exhausts, reflected back from the ground. As the Harrier GR.Mk.5, this reworked aircraft would be able to carry 1,500lb more fuel or stores than the GR.Mk.3, or 3,000lb from a 1,000ft STO ground run. Manoeuvrability (particularly turning ability) was also improved. However, while Hawker Siddeley was investigating Big Wing's potential, other developments were taking place in the US where McDonnell Douglas was also pursuing the possibility of improving the performance of the existing Harrier, rather

Pictured during the Falklands Conflict, a Sea Harrier FRS.Mk.1 comes into the hover, carrying Sidewinder missiles, external fuel tanks and Aden gun pods. (Royal Navy)

HMS *Hermes*, back in Portsmouth at the conclusion of the Falklands Conflict in 1982. Sea Harriers are lined-up on deck, prior to their short flight back to their base at Yeovilton. Mission 'kill' markings are visible under the aircraft's cockpit. (*Aeroplane*)

A colourful scene at RNAS Yeovilton, with No 899 NAS's Sea Harriers out on the flight line, illuminated by some evening sunshine. (Rich Pittman)

than creating an entirely new one from scratch. Mindful of Kingston's activities, the American design team accepted that a new wing design was the key to creating a far more capable aircraft. Likewise, they concluded that an improved engine combined with a completely new intake design (with two rows of pressure recovery inlet doors) would enable the thrust of the Pegasus 103 to be increased by more than 500lb. McDonnell Douglas also embraced Kingston's lift improvement devices for the lower fuselage and the result was the AV-8B; a direct development of the first-generation Harrier that greatly improved capability. Of course, it was not drastically different from the Harrier GR.Mk.5 being proposed by Hawker Siddeley at Kingston and Britain was therefore left with a choice between continuing to develop the Big Wing GR.Mk.5, buying the American-designed AV-8B, or doing nothing at all and simply updating the existing Harrier fleet more modestly. The prospect of adopting the AV-8B was less than popular, not least because it looked as if Britain would be re-importing its own technology. On the other hand, the GR.Mk.5 project was undoubtedly less ambitious but significantly more expensive, and America would pay most of the bill for creating the AV-8B. Eventually, it was agreed that an all-British programme was unnecessarily expensive and that the GR.Mk.5 would be dropped. A Memorandum of Understanding was signed in August 1981 to purchase the American AV-8B, incorporating some small

modifications (such as additional pylons for Sidewinder missiles) catered to RAF requirements. This new design would then become the Harrier GR.Mk.5. The AV-8B agreement divided the manufacture of the aircraft between the US and the UK, with McDonnell Douglas responsible for 60 per cent of the airframe (in terms of man hours) while British Aerospace would be responsible for the remaining 40 per cent, particularly the rear fuselage, tailplanes and the rudder assembly. Each nation would then complete the assembly of their own aircraft, combining the components from each company, and incorporating the avionics and other modifications peculiar to each variant. A similar arrangement was established between Rolls-Royce and Pratt & Whitney, with Rolls-Royce responsible for 75 per cent of the engine manufacture, and all of the final assembly. The first six completed rear fuselage sections were duly supplied by BAe to the US and these were incorporated into the first four Full Scale Development (FSD) airframes (161396 to 161399), together with a pair of non-flying test specimens.

Although retaining most of the original Harrier's basic configuration, the AV-8B was very much a new design, built around a new 28ft wing that was, at that time, the largest structure to have been manufactured from carbon fibre composite materials. Some 300lb lighter than the equivalent metal structure, it was also a staggering 400 per cent stronger. Incorporated into the wing were new single-slot flaps that circulated some of the engine exhaust flow when lowered, adding 7,600lb of lift during STO. Added to this was the additional lift created by the new under-fuselage modifications and more improvements to overall manoeuvrability created by wing Leading Edge Root Extensions (LERX) that were eventually incorporated mostly in response to RAF demands for better agility. The larger wing enabled six weapons pylons to be fitted and the greater span enabled the RCV nozzles to be positioned further outboard, thereby improving lateral control without compromising engine bleed thrust. The forward fuselage was redesigned along similar lines to the Sea Harrier with a new raised cockpit, combined with a larger (bubbled) canopy that greatly improved all-round vision. Oddly, the outrigger wheels were moved slightly inboard and, although this might have been seen as a retrograde step in terms of ground stability, it would enable the aircraft to operate successfully from smaller single-track roads when necessary. In essence, McDonnell Douglas had created a brilliant compromise design that provided many of the improvements of the abortive AV-16 whilst still retaining the original Harrier's configuration. Formal US approval for the aircraft was issued on 27 July 1976 and the 'Harrier II' was born. A redundant AV-8A (158385) was rebuilt to AV-8B aerodynamic standards for wind tunnel tests at NASA's Ames Research Center, two complete prototypes were manufactured from AV-8As 158394 and 158395, although they were only partially rebuilt, retaining the AV-8A's original nose section and shorter fuselage. They were, however, fitted with the new YF402-RR-404 engines and new redesigned 'zero-scarf' nozzles that fully enclosed the engine exhaust and prevented any of the engine thrust from splaying outwards, thereby increasing the engine's lift properties. The first of the prototypes took to the air on 19 February 1979 but its initial flight-testing programme was cut short when an engine flame-out resulted in the aircraft being lost on 15 November (the pilot ejected to safety). The prototypes proved the validity of the AV-8B design, although to some extent, the design teams were disappointed by the aircraft's slightly inferior speed performance, created by greater drag. Despite various attempts to improve this deficiency, the USMC expressed satisfaction with the aircraft's overall performance, and with much better range, manoeuvrability and payload capability, it was accepted that a slight reduction in top speed was an acceptable compromise (flat-out speed was never a priority for the USMC). The first of the FSD aircraft achieved its first flight on 5 November 1981 (flown by Charles A. Plummer) and the second and third aircraft followed on 7 and 10 April of the following year. The fourth aircraft made its maiden flight on 4 June 1983. The first two aircraft were fitted with instrumentation nose booms, while the second pair received wing LERX modifications, this being a '70 per cent LERX' as opposed to a '100 per cent' derivative that appeared later. The last of the four FSD machines was completed to a more definitive standard and assigned to weapons release testing, including the new 25mm cannon that had been created for the AV-8B. The earlier Aden 30mm cannon had already proved to be very effective and reliable but as a British design, supply of components and ammunition had always been a headache. The new cannon comprised a GAU-12/U weapon housed in the left-hand gun pod, while the right-hand pod was used to house the ammunition, a 'bridge' across the lower fuselage to feed the gun being part of the design. With a firing rate of 3,600 rounds per minute, it was similar to cannon fitted to USMC armoured vehicles, and this enabled a degree of commonality to be introduced. The same Hughes ASB-19(V)-2 Angle Rate Bombing System (ARBS) used in the A-4 Skyhawk was incorporated into the new design, linked to a mission computer (AYK-14) and a HUD. This system was designed to use collimated TV and laser spot-trackers (located in the aircraft's nose) to give the pilot a magnified (up to 6x) view on the pilot's display inside the cockpit, where the instrument layout was a generational leap from the earlier Harrier. Instead of a jumble of analogue instrumentation (little different from the equipment fitted to the aged Hawker Hunter) the new aircraft had multi-function display screens and a Hands On Throttle And Stick (HOTAS) system very similar to that fitted to the USMC's Hornets. A three-axis Sperry stability augmentation and attitude

Above: Sea Harrier FA.Mk.2 ZH813 was the last new-build Mk.2 variant delivered to the Royal Navy (on 18 January 1999). After retirement, it was assigned to RNAS Culdrose as a ground instructional airframe. (Key Collection)

Below and overleaf: No 899 NAS celebrated the impending retirement of the Sea Harrier (and 25 years of operations on the type) by painting FA.Mk.2 ZH809 in what was evidently meant to be a recreation of the Sea Harrier FRS.Mk.1's delivery paint scheme. The result was certainly eye-catching, not least because the aircraft's upper surfaces were painted a vivid shade of blue rather than Dark Sea Grey. In typical flamboyant FAA fashion, the aircraft's undersides were also suitably decorated. (Tom Cheney and Key Collection)

hold system (SAAHS) was also fitted, giving the pilot a much easier workload when operating the aircraft in the hover, and while transitioning to and from wing-borne flight. The system could be used to conduct a completely 'hands-off' vertical landing if necessary. This was ably demonstrated in February 1983 when test pilot Bill Lowe performed such a manoeuvre. Although not applicable to routine flying, it did demonstrate just how much automation was available to the pilot and how the challenging task of handling the Harrier had been significantly improved.

Chapter 5

Second Generation Woes

The first production AV-8B (161573) made its first flight on 29 August 1983. Although the design of the aircraft had been continually refined up until the completion of the first production aircraft, the aircraft had in fact changed little since the beginning of the design process. The only obvious external alteration was the deletion of the new twinset of blow-in doors, following another redesign of the ever-challenging inlet area. With the internal ducting re-contoured again, the design reverted to the more traditional single row of doors, similar to those found on first-generation Harriers. Production of dual-control derivatives of the AV-8B seemed certain but initially the USMC was reluctant to order any aircraft, believing that conversion training to the new Harrier could be completed on the original TAV-8A airframes, the basic handling of the aircraft being virtually identical in most respects. However, the all-new cockpit with digital instrumentation was completely different to that found in the existing trainers, and students were not able to make the transition to the new aircraft without some difficulty. Therefore, it was eventually decided that eight of the AV-8B aircraft on order would be cancelled, enabling funds to be shifted to the purchase of the TAV-8B. Some 28 aircraft were purchased, the first of these making its maiden flight on 21 October 1986. As with the creation of the Harrier T.Mk.2, the TAV-8B is essentially a standard AV-8B with a redesigned nose section, accommodating a second raised cockpit and a slightly larger fin area. The fuselage was also increased in length by some 3ft 11in and this made an extended tail boom unnecessary. The only other significant alteration to the design was the deletion of stores points, and only two weapons pylons were fitted, which were used for training stores or external fuel tanks (there was no intention to 'dual role' the aircraft as an operationally capable aircraft). The first AV-8Bs entered USMC service in January 1985 when VMA-331 retired their A-4 Skyhawks.

Meanwhile, Britain was also preparing to introduce its own version of this second-generation Harrier. British Aerospace reached an agreement to provide 40 per cent of all AV-8B airframe manufacture and 50 per cent in the case of the RAF's Harrier GR.Mk.5, and the RAF ordered 60 aircraft, the first (ZD318) making its first flight at Dunsfold on 30 April 1985. Service deliveries began on 29 May 1987, when ZD325 arrived at RAF Wittering for engineering familiarisation. The OCU training courses shifted to the GR.Mk.5 in July 1988 and No 1 Squadron became the first operational Harrier GR.Mk.5 unit on 2 November 1989. No 3 and 4 Squadrons then re-equipped with the type, leaving only the continuing Belize detachment operating the increasingly elderly Harrier GR.Mk.3. Although manufacture of the AV-8B and Harrier GR5 was a shared experience (with components going across the Atlantic in both directions), the RAF's Harrier was substantially different to the AV-8B. While the USMC wanted a relatively simple and rugged CAS aircraft, the RAF wanted something more versatile and capable (now referred to as a Battlefield Air Interdiction aircraft) that could operate against second and third-echelon forces. As a result, the GR.Mk.5 was significantly heavier than its American counterpart. The GR.Mk.5 cockpit included a Smiths SU-128/A HUD, a Hughes ASB-19 Angle Rate Bombing Set, and a Ferranti moving map display. Marconi Zeus RWR equipment was incorporated together with a Plessey Missile Approach Warning System (MAWS). ALE-40 expendable countermeasures (chaff and flares) were also included and the AV-8B's Litton ASN-130 INS was adopted, in preference to the planned Ferranti FIN.1075 (although this was eventually retrofitted). The Rolls-Royce Pegasus Mk.105 engine took advantage of a new Digital Engine Control System (DECS) that improved engine operation and provided smooth reliability throughout the engine's parameters (it was also incorporated into the Pegasus engines

It is perhaps inevitable that the Harrier will chiefly be remembered for its public demonstrations, in which the aircraft's hover capabilities captured the attention of spectators. The RAF routinely sanctioned an annual solo Harrier display routine for the airshow season throughout the aircraft's tenure of service with the RAF. Most displays traditionally ended with a graceful bow towards the crowd. (Key Collection)

An AV-8B pictured at China Lake NAS in April 1989 during night attack systems trials. (US Navy)

installed in the AV-8Bs). The GR.Mk.5's weapon pylons were also different to those fitted to the AV-8B. The RAF's use of the BL.755 cluster bomb (bigger and heavier than the USMC's 'standard' Mk.82 bomb) required redesigned pylons, and an additional outer pylon was also fitted for the carriage of Sidewinder missiles. Although this outer pylon was not capable of carrying anything else, it did of course free the other pylons to carry heavier ordnance. The USMC's 25mm cannon was not adopted, nor was the older Aden 30mm cannon. Instead, a new gas-operated Aden 25mm cannon was selected that provided a much better rate of fire and higher muzzle velocity. However, development of the new cannon was troublesome and, by 1999, these difficulties (compounded by increasing cost) led to the cannon being abandoned. Because the gun pods contributed to the Harrier's lift, they were still carried under the aircraft, but only rarely did they actually carry equipment, and it is doubtful whether any were ever actually fired. Also unique to the GR.Mk.5 was the distinctive 'chisel' fairing under the extreme nose that was to have housed a Miniature Infra-red Line Scan Equipment (MIRLS) system. Cost overruns eventually led to the equipment being cancelled, but by this time, the Harrier's nose was already being manufactured and so the redundant fairing survived, endowing the aircraft with a unique nose profile that ultimately served no practical purpose.

The first major development of the second-generation Harrier was the creation of a night attack variant for the USMC, originally referred to as the AV-8D but later redesignated as the AV-8B(NA). Testing of a GEC-Marconi Forward Looking Infrared (FLIR) system and GEC 'Cats Eyes' night-vision goggles (NVGs) was conducted at China Lake, leading to equipment being incorporated into modified aircraft, and resulting in a distinctive fairing appearing above the aircraft's nose cone. Also incorporated into the AV-8B(NA) was a new wide-field HUD, colour MFD screens, a digital map display and additional chaff/flare dispensers attached to the upper fuselage. The RAF's LERX was also fitted and the leading edge of the lower fin redesigned to incorporate a modified ram air intake. The prototype for this new configuration was AV-8B 162966, which flew as an AV-8B(NA) for the first time on 26 June 1987, and subsequent production aircraft were then completed to this standard. The first operational aircraft became available

A pair of AV-8B Harriers from VMA-211, the 'Wake Island Avengers'. Together, the aircraft are carrying a wide range of standard weaponry, comprising of cannon packs, Sidewinders, Snakeye retarded HE bombs and rocket pods. (USMC)

in September 1989. The second major development was the Harrier II Plus, derived from a design first created by McDonnell Douglas in 1987 (then referred to as the AV-8E). With a more powerful Pegasus engine, the E-model was designed to incorporate a new radar system with both air-to-air and air-to-ground modes. Interest in the project dwindled (largely due to budget restraints) but it re-emerged in 1988, when BAe and McDonnell Douglas announced a private venture project to develop this design. Both Spain and Italy expressed interest in the proposal and eventually a four-nation deal was established with both Alenia and CASA taking a 15 per cent share of the programme. Of course, this was not the first Harrier variant to carry radar, as the hugely successful Sea Harrier FA.Mk.2 was employing the GEC-Marconi Blue Vixen system and it seemed logical that this equipment would be used for the AV-8B. Indeed, it was suggested that the same radar should also be retrofitted to USMC Hornets, as it was proving to be an excellent piece of kit, integrated with the equally successful AIM-20 missile. Sadly, cost considerations precluded the notion of re-equipping the Hornet squadrons and the Hughes APG-73 was chosen for this aircraft instead. This effectively freed the Hornet's older APG-65 radar and this was then

AV-8B 162722 from VMA-331, wearing Gulf War grey/blue camouflage. The unit flew some 242 combat sorties during Operation *Desert Storm*. (Mick Roth Collection)

AV-8B Plus Harriers on VMA-542's flight line. The 'Flying Tigers' was the first to convert to the AV-8B Plus variant, deliveries beginning in July 1993. (US Navy)

Pictured at El Centro NAS, this angle of the TAV-8B illustrates the unusual proportions of the type's tail fin. Unlike the first generation T2/4, which incorporated a longer tail boom and taller fin, the TAV-8B incorporates a broader chord and higher fin with a downward-stepped leading edge. (Gary Wetzel)

Although VMAT-203 is more generally associated with the dual control TAV-8B (as the USMC's Harrier training unit), a number of single-seat AV-8B aircraft are also operated by the unit, including this specially marked machine with a celebratory tail decoration. (Lance Pawlik)

used for the AV-8B. The resulting aircraft (the AV-8B Harrier II Plus) is in effect the AV-8B(NA) with radar housed in a redesigned forward nose section, embracing all of the modifications previously made to the night attack variant. With existing AV-8B aircraft gradually being brought up to this standard, the AV-8B Plus became the USMC's standard Harrier variant, embracing all of the technological improvements developed over the preceding years plus more recent innovations such as GPS, a digital targeting data link, the Litening II Targeting Pod system and new precision-guided munitions. The RAF also acquired some of the AV-8B developments, most notably the same night attack system, and this formed the basis of the Harrier GR.Mk.7. When the initial purchase of the Harrier GR.Mk.5 was made in 1988, options on further aircraft were included and a batch of 34 Harrier GR.Mk.7s was subsequently ordered, together with a plan to modify the earlier GR.Mk.5s to the same standard. The complicated production process resulted in some of these aircraft being completed to GR.Mk.5A standard, featuring most of the later variant's modifications, pending delivery and fitments of the new avionics. When completed, these part-modified aircraft were placed in storage pending final conversion and delivery as Mk.7s. Harrier ZD318 became the prototype GR.Mk.7 and flew for the first time in this configuration on 20 November 1989. Distinguishable from the GR.Mk.5 by virtue of a redesigned nose section, the GR.Mk.7 featured a nose-top GEC-Marconi 1010 FLIR fairing (similar to that found on the AV-8B) and new under-nose fairings for the Marconi-Zeus ECM system. In other respects, the aircraft was similar to the GR.Mk.5, although from the 17th new-build aircraft onwards, the LERX was switched to the later '100 per cent' design (with deeper cross section and reshaped dimensions). This was progressively retrofitted to earlier aircraft (and most AV-8Bs) that featured the '75 per cent' LERX design. Unlike the USMC AV-8B(NA), the Harrier GR.Mk.7 took advantage of an ingenious compressed air jettisoning system that ensured safe separation of the pilot's NVGs before ejection. It was envisaged that night-attack equipment could also be fitted to existing Harrier T.Mk.4 trainers (creating what would have been the Harrier Mk.6). But eventually, the RAF received 13 Harrier Mk.10 aircraft that were essentially standard TAV-8B models with GR.Mk.7 equipment, thereby retaining the dual training and combat capability preferred by the RAF (the Mk.6 would have presented the RAF with the logistical difficulties of supporting only a small fleet of first-generation Harriers that were to be used only for training). The first Harrier T.Mk.10 (ZH653) was assembled at Dunsfold and made its first flight there on 7 April 1994, although subsequent aircraft were assembled at Warton (Dunsfold was committed to Sea Harrier work at this time). The first Harrier T10 was delivered to the RAF on 30 January 1995. The final stage of the RAF's programme of modifications was the GR.Mk.9, which was a significantly updated development of the GR.Mk.7, incorporating the ability to use a wide range of advanced precision weaponry, new communications, and systems and airframe upgrades. Integration and clearance of these weapons enabled the RAF's crews to hit a wider range of targets harder, at longer range and with less risk to pilots. The first of these improved aircraft equipped the new Joint Force Harrier (JFH) squadrons crewed by both RAF and Royal Navy personnel, following the withdrawal of the Royal Navy's Sea Harriers. The JFH concept created a merged capability between the two services, comprising a force of four frontline squadrons and one OCU. The RAF supplied air and ground crew for two of the squadrons and the RN for the other two, while the OCU was jointly crewed. Operations were concentrated at the RAF's bases at Cottesmore and Wittering, with training activities largely confined to the latter base, and units deploying to sea on a regular basis. Alongside the GR.Mk.9 upgrade programme, aircraft were fitted with more powerful engines to enable them to perform more efficiently in extremely hot climates. Aircraft with the improved engines were designated GR.Mk.9A. Under a £100m contract awarded to BAE Systems in 2004, new digital weapons integrated into the GR.Mk.9 included an advanced Global Positioning System and laser guided Paveway IV bomb, and infrared and television variants of the Maverick missile to achieve high precision ground attack capabilities. The aircraft was also cleared to carry up to six Paveway IV bombs, linked by a new onboard computer. The Successor Identification Friend or Foe system (IFF) also enhanced the aircraft's versatility, making it less vulnerable on operational missions. The aircraft was later fitted to carry the advanced Brimstone anti-armour missile. Part of longer-term plans for the aircraft included secure communications, a ground proximity warning system and for training, the Rangeless Airborne Instrumentation and Debriefing System (RAIDS). The programme also extended to an equivalent upgrade for the trainer aircraft to T.Mk.12 standard. Joint Force Harrier was expected to remain in service until 2015, when deliveries of the Lockheed Martin F-35 would begin. However, Britain's dire financial situation forced another round of defence cuts and high on the list of potential savings was JFH. Despite commitments in theatres such as Afghanistan, the British Ministry of Defence concluded (in October 2010) that the purchase of two new aircraft carriers should go ahead and that the entire Harrier fleet would be withdrawn with immediate effect. The decision was met with disbelief both within the RAF and throughout the British media and on the day that the news was released, RAF (and FAA) Harrier operations were immediately ended, some crews literally being stopped in their tracks as they prepared to fly training missions. Harriers would be withdrawn from service completely by April 2011, although in a matter of days from the announcement, it became clear that most operations would effectively come to an end in December 2010, even though there was no prospect of F-35s coming into service for at least another five years.

During December 2010, HMS *Ark Royal*'s final deployment of Harriers ended, and the mighty ship sailed into Portsmouth for retirement. On 15 December, JFH flew a magnificent 16-aircraft formation of Harriers to mark the aircraft's retirement from RAF and Royal Navy service. The flypast was to have been repeated the following day but miserable weather conditions resulted in the Harriers returning to Cottesmore in groups of four, to make individual short and vertical landings before assembled crowds. At 1440hrs, Cottesmore's station commander brought the last Harrier

Factory fresh Harrier GR5s pictured shortly after delivery to No 233 OCU at Wittering. (Tim McLelland)

No 4 Squadron's ZD346 pictured just seconds before touchdown at Cottesmore, just weeks before the type's retirement in 2010. (Rich Pittman)

ZG512, a Harrier GR9 from No 1 Squadron, pictured at low level over the snowy hills of Wales during a training sortie in 2010. (Rich Pittman)

back for a final bow and landing (vertically, of course) to mark the end of the very last Harrier sortie. The Harrier pilots then returned to their waiting families (accompanied by a pipe band) and with more than a touch of sadness and partial disbelief, the long story of Britain's association with the Harrier was effectively over.

Far beyond British shores, the Harrier remained in business. Spain ordered 12 AV-8B second-generation Harriers (designated as the VA.2) and these were flown directly to Spain during 1987. In 1990, Spain entered into an agreement with the US to produce the Harrier II+ derivative, incorporating APG-65 radar and night-vision capability. From the existing fleet, ten aircraft were subsequently converted to this standard and a further eight new-build aircraft were ordered, enabling Spain to retire the first-generation AV-8S aircraft. Operating at sea from the Navy's carrier *Dedalo* until 1988, a new carrier (*Principe de Astrurias*) entered service in 1989, with facilities to handle eight Harriers, including a 12-degree launch ramp from the outset (the previous carrier was never fitted with a ramp). Although the integration of modern weapons systems was slow, the Navy's Harriers became the most capable aircraft in Spain's military inventory, and they look set to remain in service for many more years, with no plans for any replacement programme having yet been made. India's interest in the Harrier emerged in 1978 when plans were drawn up for a modern carrier force that would be equipped with 48 Harriers. These would be export versions of the Royal Navy's Sea Harrier (the Mk.51). The first six aircraft (together with a pair of T.Mk.60 trainer derivatives) were ordered in December 1979, the first aircraft taking to the air in August 1982. The new aircraft were initially delivered to Yeovilton where crew conversion training took place and the first three aircraft departed for India on 13 December 1983. The projected second order for an additional four aircraft was cancelled but, in November 1985, a further ten single-seat and

Harrier GR.Mk.9 aircraft from No 1 Squadron, pictured returning from an exercise in Norway, complete with 'winter' camouflage comprising of temporary white paint applied over the aircraft's standard grey finish. With a full complement of external fuel tanks for the long ferry flight home, the aircraft's refuelling probes are extended, ready to take on fuel from a VC10 tanker. (Key Collection)

one twin-seat aircraft were ordered. A third batch of seven single-seat aircraft (and another trainer) was placed in 1986, bringing the total order up to 23 single-seat machines and four dual-control variants. India now operates the only surviving examples of the Sea Harrier, together with the T.60 trainers that were based on the RAF's T.Mk.4 airframe. Two attrition replacements were purchased, these being former RAF aircraft that were refurbished prior to delivery. Equipped with the Sea Eagle missile, the Sea Harrier provides India's Navy with an aged but still very effective fighting machine. Upgraded with a new Elta EL/M-2032 radar and Rafael Derby BVRAAMs, the Sea Harrier fleet will eventually be replaced by MiG-29K fighters, although the timescale for this transition remains unclear. Italy's interest in the Harrier emerged in 1967 when Hugh Merewether landed a pre-production aircraft on the Italian Navy's *Andrea Doria* helicopter carrier. It was envisaged that six Mk.50 aircraft would be purchased while a further 44 would be licence-assembled in Italy, however, cost considerations combined with political opposition (compounded by a 1937 treaty that prohibited the Italian Navy from flying fixed-wing aircraft) eventually led to the abandonment of these plans. When a new helicopter carrier (the *Giuseppe Garibaldi*) was launched in 1983, it was clear that Italy still intended to acquire fixed-wing aircraft of some description as the vessel incorporated a 'ski jump' ramp in its design. Following evaluation of both the Sea Harrier and AV-8B, Italy finally ordered two TAV-8B trainer aircraft in May 1989. Some 16 AV-8B+ aircraft were then ordered with options on a further eight machines. The first aircraft were taken from the USMC order and went directly to Cherry Point for conversion training, while the rest were assembled in Italy.

Below and overleaf: In 1979, India placed its first order for six Sea Harriers, the first three of which arrived at Dabolim Airport on 16 December 1983. A separate deal for another ten Sea Harriers followed in November 1985; eventually a total of 30 Harriers was procured, 25 for operational use and the remainder as dual-seat trainer aircraft. India has operated its Sea Harriers from the aircraft carriers INS *Vikrant* and INS *Viraat* (formerly HMS *Hermes*). There have been a significant number of accidents involving the Sea Harrier, which caused approximately half of the fleet to be lost. Surviving aircraft were upgraded in collaboration with Israel, installing the Elta EL/M-2032 radar and the Rafael Derby BVR missile. (Tim McLelland Collection)

54
NAVY

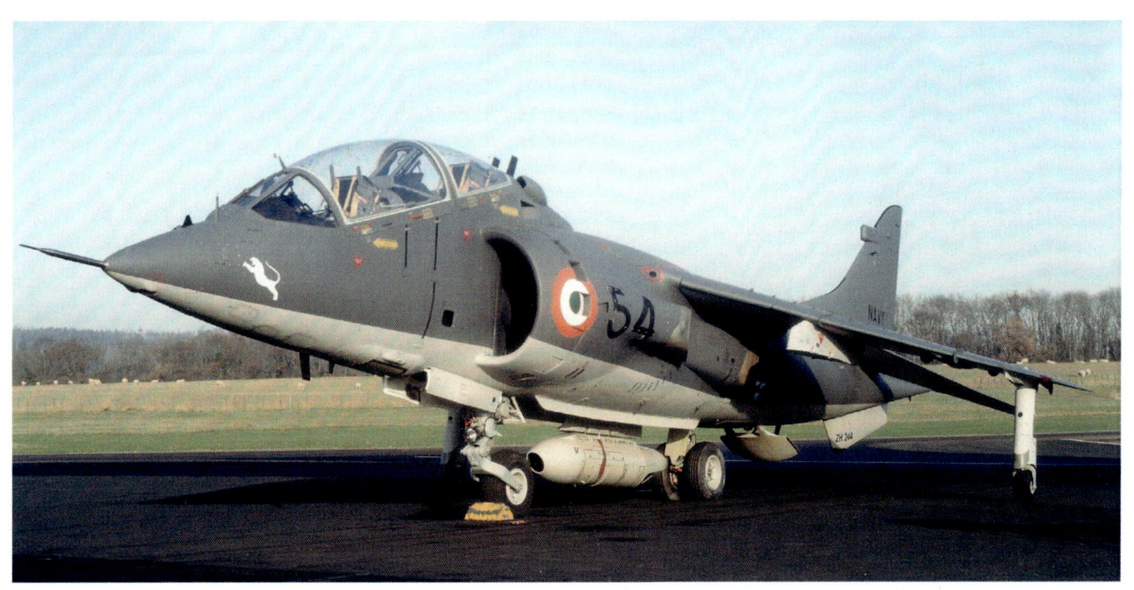

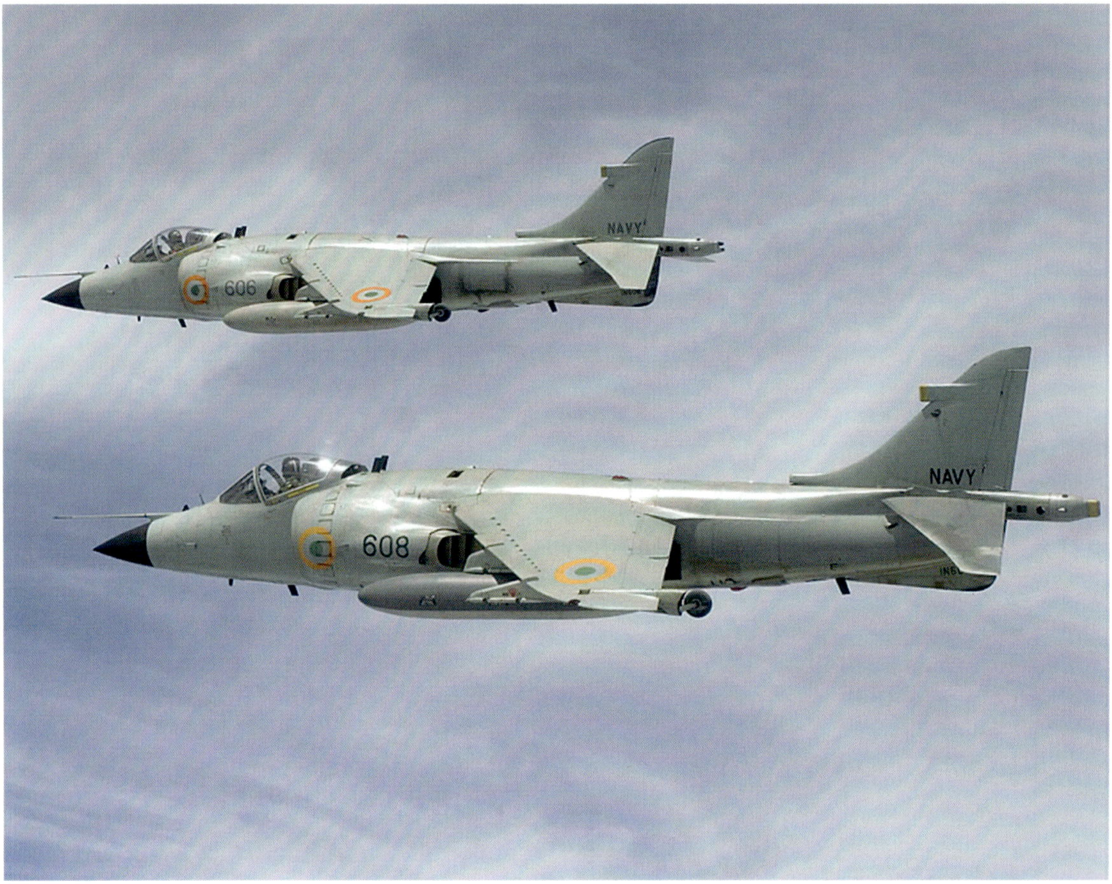
NAVY
606
NAVY
608

Above, below and overleaf: Thailand operated only ten Harriers, which it had acquired from Spain when that country's air arm re-equipped with more modern AV-8B aircraft. The fleet of AV-8S and twin-seat TAV-8S aircraft were acquired to operate from the Royal Thai Navy's aircraft carrier HMS *Chakri Naruebet*, although funding issues prevent the aircraft from deploying on a regular basis, and the aircraft were usually shore based. The lack of funding and a spares shortage had a severe effect upon the Harrier force and, by 1999, it is believed that only one aircraft was combat-ready. Not surprisingly, the Harriers were gradually withdrawn from use, the last examples having been retired in 2006. (Tim McLelland Collection)

Above, below and overleaf: Spain operated ten export versions of the Harrier GR.Mk.1, designated as the AV-8S Matador. When these aircraft approached the end of their useful lives, Spain became the first international operator of the AV-8B by signing an order for 12 aircraft in March 1983. Designated VA-2 Matador II by the Spanish Navy (Armada Española), this variant is known as EAV-8B by McDonnell Douglas. On 6 October 1987, the first three Matador IIs were delivered to Naval Station Rota and deliveries were complete by 1988. BAe test pilots cleared the aircraft carrier *Principe de Asturias* for Harrier operations in July 1989. 9a Escuadrilla was formed on 29 September 1987 to become part of the Alpha Carrier Air Group and operate the EAV-8B. In March 1993, under the September 1990 Tripartite MoU between the US, Italy, and Spain, eight EAV-8B Plus Matadors were ordered, along with a twin-seat TAV-8B. On 11 May 2000, Boeing and the NAVAIR finalised a contract to re-manufacture Spanish EAV-8Bs to bring them up to AV-8B Plus standard. Eventually, five aircraft were modified, the last being delivered on 5 December 2003. Spanish EAV-8Bs joined Operation *Deny Flight*, enforcing the UN's no-fly zone over Bosnia and Herzegovina. Following the decommissioning of the *Príncipe de Asturias* in February 2013, the sole naval platform from which Spanish Harrier IIs can operate is the *Juan Carlos* amphibious assault ship. (Andre Jans, Erik Roelofs and *Aeroplane*)

Following a lengthy evaluation of the Sea Harrier and AV-8B, an order was placed for two TAV-8Bs in May 1989 followed by a contract for 16 AV-8B Plus aircraft. The twin-seaters arrived at Grottaglie in August 1991 and, in 1994, the initial batch of US-built aircraft arrived at MCAS Cherry Point for pilot conversion training. The first Italian-assembled Harrier was rolled out the following year. During January 1995, *Giuseppe Garibaldi* deployed to Somalia with three Harriers on board, to maintain stability following the withdrawal of UN forces, returning to port on 22 March. Italian AV-8Bs were used for the first time in combat missions during 1999, when they were deployed aboard *Giuseppe Garibaldi*, participating in Operation *Allied Force* in Kosovo. Italian pilots conducted more than 60 sorties, using conventional and laser-guided bombs. From November 2001, eight AV-8Bs were deployed to the Indian Ocean in support of Operation *Enduring Freedom*. Operating throughout January and February 2002, some 131 missions were logged for a total of 647 flight hours. In 2011, Italian Harriers worked alongside aircraft of other nations during Operation *Unified Protector*, as part of the 2011 military intervention in Libya. They conducted airstrikes as well as intelligence and reconnaissance sorties over Libya, using the LITENING targeting pods while armed with AIM-120 AMRAAMs and AIM-9 Sidewinders. (Michael Balter)

Other books you might like:

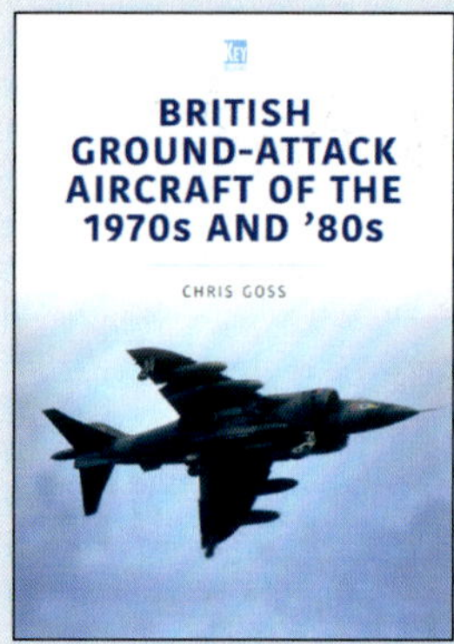

Historic Military Aircraft Series, Vol. 8

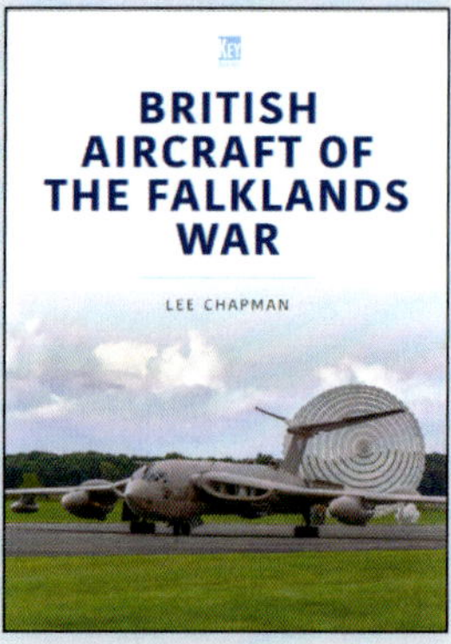

Historic Military Aircraft Series, Vol. 13

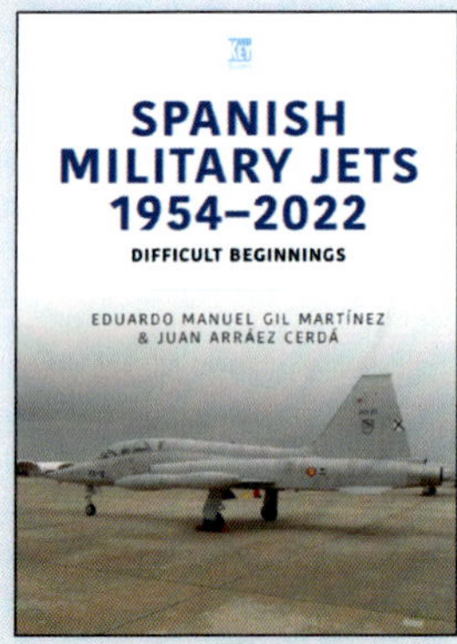

Modern Military Aircraft Series, Vol. 9

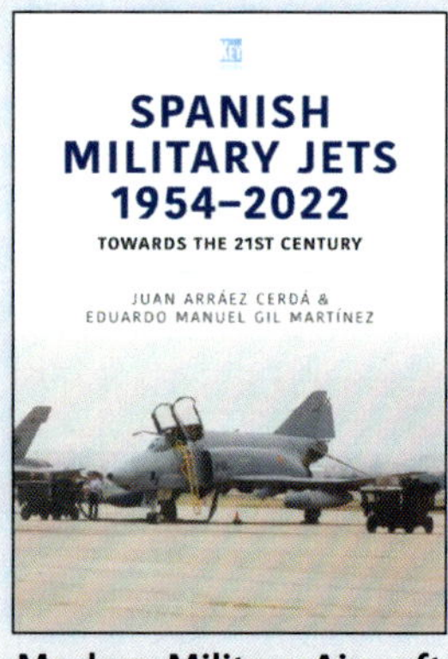

Modern Military Aircraft Series, Vol. 10

Historic Military Aircraft Series, Vol. 16

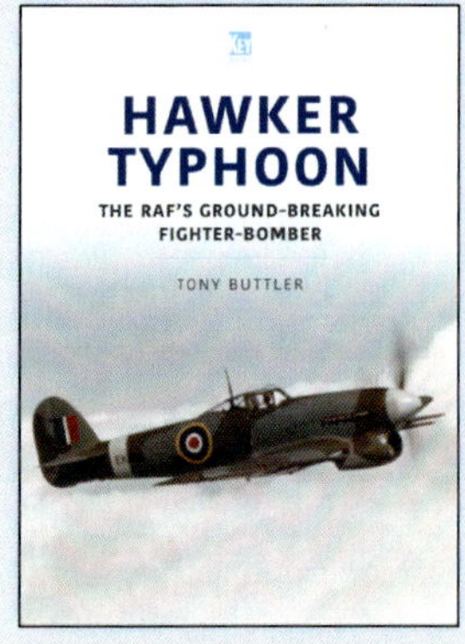

Historic Military Aircraft Series, Vol. 5

For our full range of titles please visit:

shop.keypublishing.com/books

VIP Book Club

Sign up today and receive
TWO FREE E-BOOKS

Be the first to find out about our forthcoming book releases and receive exclusive offers.

Register now at **keypublishing.com/vip-book-club**

*Our VIP Book Club is a 100% spam-free zone, and we will never share your email with anyone else.
You can read our full privacy policy at: privacy.keypublishing.com*